tapas bar

The managing editors wish to thank Édouard Collet, Christine Martin, and Mélanie Joly for their valuable aid and Marine Barbier for her careful reading.

casual spanish cooking at home

tapas bar

Sophie Brissaud

Photographs by Yves Bagros
Design by Laurence du Tilly

[when the flavors blend...]

To everyone's delight, national borders are slowly disappearing in matters of cuisine. As the new century gets underway, we're witnessing a gradual acceptance of new culinary habits. We don't talk about "exotic cuisine" anymore because exotic means faraway, strange, and not necessarily authentic. We no longer consider Chinese, Indian, or Mexican food to be unusual fare. The sources of inspiration for our cooking no longer matter as long as the results are delicious. It used to be that trying our hand at foreign cuisine was considered audacious, even daring, but today it's part of our everyday lives. Ingredients that, in the past, had to be tracked down with the skill of a detective or brought back by travelling friends, are now available locally from the neighborhood supermarket or even our corner grocer. We are no longer intimidated by peculiar spices, mysterious jars of ingredients, or colorful fruits—but instead we are learning how to use them. The world is coming to us and its flavors are being awakened in our kitchens. At the same time, we're discovering different ways of eating as well as new dietary principles and eating habits from other countries. Our kitchens have become the melting pot for a natural blending of tastes; what was once quite curious is now so familiar that we forget its origins are foreign.

Just ten or twenty years ago, no one was talking about Spanish cuisine except when referring to paella or to a cuisine using lots of oil, imagined to be too rich. Times have certainly changed! Now everyone recognizes the excellence of Spanish cuisine. Dried Iberian hams are considered the best (and most expensive) in the world. Olive oil, of which Spain is the largest European producer, has come to be recognized as the most digestible and beneficial glyceride for the human body. And best of all, we've discovered tapas, those delicious, widely varied, bite-size morsels intended for serving with drinks. Tapas bars have been popping up everywhere, but tapas taste best in their native land where people spend entire evenings snacking on them as they travel from bar to bar. The name comes from "tapa," meaning "lid" or "cover," referring to a small dish used to cover the wine glass designed to keep out flies. The same dish also held a slice of chorizo and a few olives for snacking and was passed around. Certainly, the most memorable tapas meals include a bottle of sherry. There is nothing to keep you from offering your friends an unforgettable tapas feast in your own home. The quantities in these recipes are designed for varying numbers of people, thereby allowing you to adapt your menu to your guests. The recipes chosen for this book are almost all traditional tapas, though some are derived from family recipes. Nevertheless, there are no strict rules and any dish can become a tapa if you serve it in small portions alongside other delicacies. And now, prepare to enjoy!

contents

spring 8

summer 30

fall 50

winter 72

desserts & beverages 94

appendices 116

spring

spring

the art of nibbling

As nice weather returns, so does the urge to sit outside on a café terrace and drink a glass of wine with some light tapas. Seafood and green vegetables are at their best in spring-inspired cuisine. Cold omelettes, marinated salads, and small warm dishes that the Spanish enjoy in abundance are also suitable for filling a picnic basket. And don't forget the bottle of well-chilled white wine!

Serves 6–8
Prep time: 45 minutes

6 small green bell peppers
4 medium ripe tomatoes
Sevillian olives (page 38),
pitted and chopped
2 tablespoons red wine
vinegar
¼ cup extra virgin olive oil
Salt
Hot *pimentón* (smoked
Spanish paprika; specialty
store)

[tomato and green pepper salad]

Broil bell peppers in the oven (as described on page 48). Wrap in aluminum foil and let cool. Then peel and discard interiors. Cut rest into strips, place in a shallow bowl, and salt lightly.

Scald tomatoes, peel, halve, and squeeze gently to remove seeds. Dice tomatoes and place on top of bell peppers. Add chopped olives, salt lightly, and sprinkle with a little *pimentón*. Just before serving, drizzle with oil and vinegar. Serve at room temperature.

[pork fritters]

Serves 4–6
Prep time: 45 minutes
Rising time: 90 minutes
Cooking time: 10 minutes

For the dough:
1 packet yeast
¼ cup lukewarm milk
2 cups flour
1 beaten egg
4 tablespoons butter, melted
Olive oil
Salt

For the filling:
2 tablespoons olive oil
2 large cloves garlic, finely chopped
1 large onion, finely chopped
¼ pound lean ground pork
1 small tomato, scalded, peeled, seeded, and mashed
½ teaspoon sweet or hot *pimentón* (smoked Spanish paprika; specialty store)
Oil for deep frying

Prepare the dough: Dissolve yeast in lukewarm milk and let stand for 10 minutes. In a large bowl, combine flour and 1 pinch salt. While stirring by hand, add beaten egg, melted butter, milk-yeast mixture and enough water to form a smooth, workable dough. Knead until it no longer sticks to your fingers (add a little flour if necessary). Place in a large bowl, coat with a thin layer of olive oil, cover with a cloth, and let rise for 90 minutes in a warm place until doubled in volume.

Meanwhile, prepare the filling. Heat olive oil in a frying pan (preferably cast iron) and sauté garlic and onion over low to medium-low heat for 5 minutes. Increase heat, add ground pork, and stir well to break apart lumps. When pork is cooked through and lightly browned, add crushed tomato and *pimentón* and season with salt. Cook on low another 5 minutes, then remove from heat, cover, and let cool.

When the dough has risen, shape it into 1-inch balls. Roll out each one thinly into a 2½-inch round. Place a little filling in the middle, fold up the sides, and seal the dough at the top to form little balls.

Heat oil for deep frying and fry fritters over medium heat (oil should register 350–375°F, using a deep-frying thermometer), turning occasionally until they have expanded and are golden brown. Remove with a slotted metal utensil, drain on paper towels, and serve hot.

[four-tiered omelette]

To save time, prepare all the ingredients and have them within reach along with 4 plates for the omelettes.

Rinse and pat dry mushrooms; chop finely. Peel garlic cloves and chop finely. Submerge tomatoes in boiling water for several seconds, remove peels and seeds, and mash flesh. Rinse spinach and place in a saucepan; season with salt and cook, covered, on medium for 5 minutes. Let cool, then squeeze spinach in paper towels to remove moisture; chop finely. Sauté all the spinach in a 8- to 9-inch nonstick pan with a little olive oil and one third of the garlic for 2 minutes. Beat 3 eggs and pour into pan. Cook until the surface has just set, then transfer omelette to a plate.

Start the same procedure once more, this time preparing a mushroom omelette, then a tomato omelette, then a shrimp omelette, each time sautéing the ingredients in olive oil with one third of the garlic (except don't use garlic with shrimp) and a little salt. Clean the pan well after each omelette.

Combine mayonnaise, Worcestershire sauce, and ketchup. Season with salt and pepper. Place spinach omelette on a platter and spread with a thin layer of sauce. Cover with the mushroom omelette and add another thin layer of sauce. Repeat this procedure with the shrimp omelette and then the tomato omelette. Cover with sauce and refrigerate for 2 hours. Cut into wedges and serve chilled or at room temperature with any remaining sauce.

Serves 6–8
Prep time: 1 hour
Cooking time: 20 minutes
Refrigeration time: 2 hours

1/3 pound mushrooms
3 cloves garlic
1 large ripe tomato
5 ounces fresh spinach with stems removed (weight without stems)
12 eggs
1/3 pound cooked and peeled shrimp, chopped
3/4 cup mayonnaise
1 dash Worcestershire sauce
2 tablespoons ketchup
Olive oil
Salt and freshly ground black pepper

[allioli potatoes]

Serves 4
Prep time: 30 minutes
Cooking time: 20 minutes

⅓ pound red potatoes
1 cup mayonnaise
(homemade is preferable)
4 cloves garlic, peeled (3 of
them well crushed)
2 tablespoons chopped
Italian parsley
1–2 teaspoons fresh lemon
juice or white wine vinegar
Salt and freshly ground
pepper

Rinse potatoes and boil with peels on in salted water along with the whole garlic clove. When potatoes are done (after 20–25 minutes, test with the tip of a knife), drain, peel, and cut into ¾-inch cubes. Discard the cooked whole garlic clove.

In a large bowl, combine mayonnaise, crushed garlic, and chopped parsley. Mix with a little lemon juice or vinegar. Season to taste, add cubed potatoes, stir carefully, and let stand for 30 minutes before serving at room temperature.

[shrimp "in raincoats"]

Serves 4–6
Prep time: 40 minutes
Cooking time:
2–3 minutes (shrimp),
15 minutes (sauce)

1 pound large shrimp
Juice of ½ lemon
1¼ cups flour
1 tablespoon white
wine vinegar
1 cup light-colored beer
1 egg white
Oil for frying

For the sauce:
3 ripe tomatoes
3 cloves garlic
3 tablespoons olive oil
1 sprig thyme
1 pinch sweet or hot
pimentón (smoked
Spanish paprika)
1 pinch sugar
Salt

Peel shrimp, leaving on the tails. Slit them down the back and remove dark-colored vein. Drizzle shrimp with a little fresh lemon juice and set aside.

Prepare the sauce: Submerge tomatoes in boiling water for several seconds, remove peels and seeds, and mash flesh. Peel and chop garlic. In a pan, heat olive oil and sauté garlic with the thyme sprig. Add tomatoes, season with salt and *pimentón*, and add sugar. Gently simmer, covered, for about 5 minutes. Remove thyme, transfer the mixture to a small bowl, and set aside.

Heat oil for frying (oil should register 350–375°F, using a deep-frying thermometer). Combine flour and salt. Gradually add vinegar and beer while stirring constantly to prevent lumps. The result should be a relatively thick batter. Beat egg white into stiff peaks and fold into batter. Hold each shrimp by the tail, dip it into the batter, and then drop it in the hot oil, cooking until golden. Fry shrimp in batches and drain on a paper towel-lined plate. Serve hot with the sauce alongside.

[garlic shrimp]

With the tip of a knife, devein shrimp. Crumble red chile pepper, if using, with your fingers (wear gloves and don't touch your face). Peel garlic cloves and slice thinly.

In a large sauté pan, heat olive oil and sauté garlic and chile pepper or *pimentón* for 1 minute. Add shrimp and stir-fry over medium heat until barely cooked (2-3 minutes). Season with salt, remove from heat, and cover immediately with a large lid or platter.

Serve at once with fresh warm bread.

Serves 6–8
Prep time: 20 minutes
Cooking time: 3 minutes

24 large raw, peeled shrimp,
fresh or frozen
1 whole spicy red chile
pepper without seeds or
½ teaspoon hot *pimentón*
(smoked Spanish paprika)
4 large cloves garlic
⅓ cup extra virgin olive oil
Salt

Serves 6–8
Prep time: 40 minutes

1 small red bell pepper
1 large ripe tomato
6 cloves garlic, peeled
1 spicy red chile pepper,
seeds removed
¼ cup red wine vinegar
⅓ cup olive oil
1 slice sourdough bread
10 blanched whole skinless
almonds
Salt and freshly ground
black pepper

[sauce romesco]

Preheat oven to 350°F for 15 minutes. Broil bell pepper, tomato, and garlic on a greased baking sheet for 12–15 minutes. Let cool. Meanwhile, marinate red chile pepper for 5 minutes in 3 tablespoons of the vinegar plus a little water.

Heat 1 tablespoon of the olive oil and lightly brown bread on both sides. Transfer bread to a paper-towel lined plate. In the same oil, toast almonds until lightly golden. Peel bell pepper and tomato and remove seeds from both.

Combine bread and chile pepper with the vinegar, toasted almonds, bell pepper, tomato, and garlic in a blender or food processor. Purée while adding remaining olive oil in a thin stream. Add remaining vinegar and season with salt and pepper.

Pour into a small bowl and serve at room temperature as an accompaniment to grilled, sautéed, or boiled shellfish (such as Garlic Shrimp on previous page).

[calamari fries]

In a sauté pan or deep fryer, heat a large amount of olive oil. You'll know it's hot enough by this test: lower a wooden spoon handle into the oil—tiny bubbles should congregate around it.

Rinse squid fillets and tentacles, pat dry, and cut fillets into rings. Dredge in flour, shaking off the excess. Deep fry squid in very hot oil (first test oil with a squid tentacle—it should sizzle immediately) until all surfaces are lightly golden, but don't let them cook too long or they'll be tough.

Drain on paper towels, salt, and serve with lemon wedges for squeezing.

Serves 4–6
Prep time: 30 minutes
Cooking time: 5 minutes

1 pound squid fillets and tentacles
Flour
Olive oil for frying
Lemons
Salt

[chicken in sparkling wine]

Cut chicken into 1/2-inch slices and then into pieces. Season with salt and pepper. Place flour in a sturdy plastic zip-top bag, add chicken, close the bag, and shake well. Remove chicken pieces from bag and shake free from excess flour.

Immediately heat olive oil in a large sauté pan and brown chicken on all sides. Add sparkling wine, then lemon juice; reduce heat and stir gently. Season with a little salt, pepper, and *pimentón*. Cover and simmer for 12–15 minutes, stirring occasionally. If the sauce evaporates or becomes too thick, add a little wine. Adjust seasonings to taste. Make sure chicken is cooked through.

Serve as part of a meal of tapas, accompanied by steamed potatoes if desired.

Serves 4
Prep time: 20 minutes
Cooking time: 12–15 minutes

2 deboned chicken legs and thighs or 2 large chicken breasts
2 tablespoons flour
1/4 cup olive oil
About 1 1/2 cups very fruity sparkling wine (Spanish cava, asti, blanquette de Limoux, or any other sparkling wine from southern France)
Juice of 1/2 lemon
Salt and freshly ground pepper
Hot *pimentón* (smoked Spanish paprika)

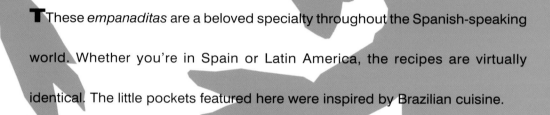

These *empanaditas* are a beloved specialty throughout the Spanish-speaking world. Whether you're in Spain or Latin America, the recipes are virtually identical. The little pockets featured here were inspired by Brazilian cuisine.

[little seafood pockets]

Serves 4–6
Prep time: 1 hour
Standing time: 1 hour
Cooking time: 1 hour

For the pastry:
2½ cups flour
½ teaspoon salt
¼ cup lard
4 tablespoons butter
2 egg yolks
¼ cup ice water
1 egg

For the filling:
2 cloves garlic
1 small onion
1 tomato
2 tablespoons olive oil
2 tablespoons flour or cornstarch
1 cup fish stock
1 pinch cumin
2 tablespoons finely chopped red bell pepper
Juice of 1 lemon
1 spicy red chile pepper without seeds and crumbled or ½ teaspoon hot *pimentón* (smoked Spanish paprika)
⅓ pound lump crabmeat or ⅓ pound raw, peeled shrimp, coarsely chopped
1 tablespoon finely chopped Italian parsley or cilantro
Salt

Sift flour into a large bowl. Add salt, lard, and butter; "cut together" using a pastry blender utensil and/or your hands until texture resembles crumbles in the size of semolina grains. Make a well in the center and add egg yolks and ice water. Combine liquid with the flour-butter mixture until the pastry has a uniform consistency. Wrap in a plastic bag and let stand in a cool place for 1 hour.

Prepare the filling: Peel and finely chop garlic and onion. Blanch tomato, peel, remove seeds, and chop flesh. Sauté onion and garlic in oil for 3 minutes on low to medium-low. Add tomato and cook on low for several minutes. Add flour or cornstarch and stir well. Add hot fish stock, while stirring, to prevent lumps. Add cumin, bell pepper, lemon juice, *pimentón*, and crabmeat or shrimp. Lightly salt and simmer over low heat for 20 minutes. Then add parsley or cilantro. The filling should be thick and creamy. Salt to taste, cover, and let cool.

Preheat oven to 325°F. Roll out pastry into a sheet about ⅛ inch thick and cut out circles 6 inches in diameter. Place 1 heaping tablespoon of filling on half of each circle. Moisten the edges of pastry, fold over to form crescents, and seal well. Brush each crescent with beaten egg and bake for about 30 minutes. Serve hot or warm.

[potato "tortilla"]

Serves 4–6
Prep time: 40 minutes
Cooking time:
About 45 minutes

1 pound Yukon gold or
fingerling potatoes
1 large onion
4 eggs
Salt and pepper
Olive oil

Peel potatoes and slice very thinly. Finely chop onion and mix with potatoes.

In a nonstick pan, heat ¼ inch olive oil and fry potatoes and onion over low heat, turning occasionally with a spatula. Handle carefully so as not to break the slices but take the time to make sure they are thoroughly cooked. (There are few things more upsetting than a potato tortilla with potatoes that aren't fully cooked.) It will take about 30 minutes. When the potatoes are done, remove them from the pan and drain well.

In a large bowl, beat eggs and gently add potatoes, salt, and pepper. Let stand for 10 minutes. Meanwhile, clean the frying pan and dry it well. Slowly heat 1 tablespoon olive oil and then add the egg-potato mixture, spreading it out over the bottom of the pan. Let the tortilla set over low heat, making sure it doesn't stick.

When the eggs are well-set and start to congeal on the surface, reverse the tortilla onto a large flat plate and slide it back into the pan to cook the other side. Let set for a few more minutes over very low heat. Cut into wedges or squares and serve hot, warm, or at room temperature. (It's best not to reheat this tortilla.)

[chicken croquettes]

After poaching, remove skin from chicken; take meat off bones and chop very finely. In a small sauté pan, heat 2 tablespoons olive oil and cook chopped chicken for about 3 minutes. Remove from heat.

Combine flour with a some of the milk, taking care to whisk out any lumps. Heat remaining milk and just before it boils, add flour-milk mixture while whisking constantly. Let thicken over low heat, cooking for 10 minutes. The sauce should be smooth. Season with salt and pepper and grate in a little nutmeg. Add chicken and simmer for another 5 minutes over low heat. Spread this mixture out in a shallow pan or bowl and let cool.

Heat oil for frying. You can check to see if it's ready by lowering a handle of a wooden spoon down into it—lots of tiny bubbles should congregate around the handle. Beat eggs in one shallow bowl and place bread crumbs in another. Shape chicken mixture into oval balls, dip in the egg, and then roll in the bread crumbs to coat. Fry in very hot oil until golden brown, in batches. Drain on a paper towel-lined plate and serve with lemon wedges.

Serves 4–6
Prep time: 40 minutes
Cooking time: 3–4 minutes

1 chicken leg and thigh or
1 large chicken breast
(poached in boiling salted
water for 30 minutes)
¼ cup flour
2 cups whole milk
2 eggs
Bread crumbs
Lemons
Olive oil for frying
Salt and pepper
Freshly-grated nutmeg

PIMENTON **PIMENTON** MENT PIMEN
AGNE QUX

Combine ingredients for vinaigrette and set aside. Beat eggs with 2 teaspoons water. Cut cheese into 1/2-inch slices, then into squares with sides about 1 inch long. Dredge cheese in flour, dip into beaten egg, and then into bread crumbs. Set aside on a plate.

In a pan, heat 1/4 inch of olive oil. When it's hot, fry the breaded cheese squares, browning well on both sides. Drain on paper towels, drizzle with vinaigrette, and serve immediately.

Serves 6
Prep time: 20 minutes
Cooking time: 4–5 minutes

2 eggs
½ pound cheese for melting
(manchego, mild Cheddar, etc.)
Flour
Bread crumbs
Olive oil

For the vinaigrette:
2 tablespoons olive oil
1 teaspoon sherry vinegar
1 finely chopped shallot
1 tablespoon finely chopped
Italian parsley
Small capers

[fried cheese]

The Conquistadors brought back many culinary treasures from the Americas,

including chile peppers. There are many varieties in Spain but pimentón

powder, available in a sweet or hot version, is the most common. It is similar

to Hungarian paprika but its flavor is less distinct. Use it according to your

fortitude and feel free to mix the two different types to accommodate your

taste and the particular recipe. Look for *pimentón* in specialty gourmet stores

or online. For Spanish tapas, its taste is unmatched.

[garlic mushrooms]

Serves 4–6
Prep time: 25 minutes
Cooking time: 15–20 minutes

Rinse and pat dry mushrooms and cut into thick slices. Peel garlic and slice.

In a sauté pan, heat oil and sauté garlic. As soon as it is evenly browned, add mushrooms and lemon juice. Stir over medium to high heat for several minutes until the moisture from the vegetables has evaporated.

Add the chile pepper, sherry, and salt; simmer for another minute. Sprinkle with chopped parsley and serve while hot.

1 pound mushrooms
6 cloves garlic
1/3 cup olive oil
Juice of 1/2 lemon
1 spicy red chile pepper without seeds and crumbled or 1/2 teaspoon hot *pimentón*
3 tablespoons dry sherry (or dry white wine)
2 tablespoons chopped Italian parsley
Salt

[seafood cocktail]

Serves 6–8
Prep time: 45 minutes
Cooking time: 10 minutes
Marinating time: 24 hours

In a covered saucepan, heat mussels, 3/4 cup water, chile, and bay leaf over high heat until mussels open, stirring once (check at the 3-minute mark). Throw away any that don't open. Don't empty the cooking liquid. Remove mussels from their shells and set aside.

In the same cooking liquid, cook unpeeled shrimp for 3 minutes over low heat and then peel. If shrimp are very large, cut into pieces. Set aside with mussels and crabmeat.

Combine sauce ingredients and pour over the shrimp, crab, and mussels. Stir gently, season to taste, cover, and marinate in the refrigerator for 24 hours.

Serve the next day, cool but not cold.

2 cups cleaned mussels
1/2 spicy red chile pepper without seeds
1 bay leaf
1 pound large shrimp
1 cup drained crabmeat

For the sauce:
1/4 cup olive oil
1/3 cup tarragon vinegar
1/4 cup chopped cornichons or pickles
2 tablespoons capers
1 finely chopped onion
1 tablespoon red bell pepper, peeled (page 48) and chopped
2 tablespoons finely chopped Italian parsley
Salt and freshly ground pepper

Serves 4–6
Prep time: 1 hour
Marinating time: 24–48 hours

1 pound large fresh anchovies (ask your fishmonger)
¾ cup sherry vinegar
4 teaspoons salt
3 cloves garlic
¾ cup fresh Italian parsley sprigs, finely chopped
Olive oil

[marinated anchovies]

Carefully rinse anchovies and separate into fillets. Dry carefully with paper towels.

Pour vinegar and ½ cup water into a non-metal bowl, add salt, and stir well until it dissolves. Place one anchovy fillet in the mixture. It should float halfway between the bottom and the surface. If the anchovy sinks, there is too much vinegar. If it floats, there is too much salt. Correct the quantities and then add remaining anchovy fillets. Cover with plastic wrap and marinate for 1–2 days in the refrigerator.

Just before serving, rinse anchovy fillets under cold running water and serve topped with finely chopped garlic and parsley—generously drizzled with olive oil. You can also serve them on hot toast rubbed with garlic.

summer

summer

cool tapas

Torrid summer is the season for cold tapas, chilled gazpacho, *escabèches* made from fresh fish, marinated vegetables, and vegetables seasoned with vinegar (eggplant, bell peppers, etc.). Summer evenings are also the time to meet with friends, enjoying dishes together that, although in other environs are considered salads or side dishes, their versatility earns them the right to be included among tapas. In summer as in every season, garlic, almonds, and saffron add a touch of Spanish refinement.

Serves 8
Prep time: 10 minutes

16 thin slices baguette (or 8
slices French bread, halved)
2 cloves garlic
2 large ripe tomatoes
16 small pieces serrano ham
Salt
Olive oil

[garlic, tomato, and serrano ham bread]

For the bread: either toast it, grill it, or fry it lightly in olive oil, on both sides.

Rub hot bread generously with garlic and then rub with a tomato half. Arrange bread on a platter, sprinkle with a little salt, drizzle with olive oil, cover with slices of serrano and serve immediately.

This tapa can be cut up into 1½-inch pieces and served with toothpicks.

[chicken in garlic sauce]

Dredge chicken pieces lightly in flour and set aside. Peel garlic cloves and keep whole.

In a sauté pan, heat olive oil and sauté garlic and chicken over medium to high heat, but don't let garlic turn too brown—remove garlic from pan as it turns golden and set aside.

Continue sautéing the chicken until all the pieces are browned evenly. Add crumbled chile and bay leaf, pour in brandy, and then flambé if desired (let flames die down before making the next addition). Then add sherry, chicken stock, and a little salt. Cover and simmer over low heat for 15 minutes.

Meanwhile, using a mortar and pestle or a food processor, process the cooked garlic, parsley, peppercorns, sea salt, and saffron if using. Add this mixture to chicken and simmer for another 15 minutes. Adjust salt to taste. Serve hot.

Serves 4–6
Prep time: 30 minutes
Cooking time: 40 minutes

1 young chicken (about 2 pounds) cut into 8 pieces (with bones)
½ cup flour
8 large cloves garlic
¼ cup olive oil
1 dried red chile pepper, without seeds and crumbled coarsely (wear gloves)
1 bay leaf
1 tablespoon brandy
¼ cup dry sherry
½ cup chicken stock
2 sprigs fresh Italian parsley
1 pinch peppercorns
1 teaspoon sea salt
1 pinch saffron threads (optional)
Salt

[fresh fish "pil-pil"]

Serves 4–6
Prep time: 40 minutes
Cooking time: 5–6 minutes

1 large very fresh hake
(about 2 pounds; ask your
fishmonger; or substitute
other fresh fish)
Juice of ½ lemon
12 cloves garlic
⅓ cup olive oil
1 teaspoon crushed red
pepper flakes (or ½
teaspoon hot *pimentón*)
2 tablespoons flour
Lemons
Fine sea salt

Have your fishmonger cut the hake into fillets and remove the bones but leave on the skin. Cut the fillet into as many pieces as you have guests. Drizzle with lemon juice, sprinkle with salt, and let stand for 30 minutes.

Peel garlic and cut into thick slices. In a pan, heat olive oil and sauté sliced garlic over medium heat. When garlic is a pale golden color, add red pepper flakes, stir for a moment, and let cook briefly over very low heat.

Pat hake fillets dry and flour lightly. Turn up the heat under the pan and fry fish fillets in oil with garlic and red pepper flakes for 2–3 minutes on each side. The fish should be well-seared but not too done. The center of the fish should still be a little translucent (it will continue to cook a bit after you remove it from the heat). Serve hot with lemon wedges.

This dish can also be prepared with salt cod or shrimp, but hake, which is more delicate, suits this recipe exceptionally well. It's a little fragile, so be careful while handling it in the pan.

[basque bell pepper omelette]

Serves 4
Prep time: 15 minutes
Cooking time: About
15 minutes

1 red bell pepper and
1 green bell pepper, both
peeled (page 48)
2 slices serrano ham
1 large onion
4 cloves garlic
3 tablespoons olive oil
2 large tomatoes, scalded,
peeled, and mashed
8 eggs
Salt and freshly ground
black pepper

Cut bell peppers and serrano ham into fine strips. Peel onion and garlic and chop both finely. In a large frying pan, sauté onion, garlic, and serrano in 2 tablespoons of the olive oil. Add tomatoes, bell peppers, salt, and pepper. Cook for 10 minutes over low to medium heat until almost all the liquid has evaporated. Transfer to a bowl.

Wipe out the pan and heat remaining oil. Beat eggs, season with salt and pepper, and pour into the hot pan. Let set over low heat for about 3 minutes while tilting the pan as necessary to distribute. When the bottom has set well, add the bell pepper-serrano mixture. Cover and cook for another 5–10 minutes over very low heat (until the egg mixture is cooked throughout). Serve hot.

[chicken pepitoria]

Serves 4–6
Prep time: 40 minutes
Cooking time: 50 minutes

2/3 cup whole almonds,
blanched and skinless
2 tablespoons flour
1 young whole chicken
(about 2 pounds) cut into
8 pieces (with bones)
1/3 cup olive oil
1 chopped onion
4 cloves garlic, chopped
1 bay leaf
3 tablespoons pine nuts
1 pinch saffron threads
2 cups dry white wine
1 hard-boiled egg
Salt and pepper

Toast almonds over low heat for 15 minutes in a dry frying pan until they change color slightly. Set aside.

Coat chicken pieces with flour (see bottom of page 18). In a sauté pan, heat half the oil and brown chicken pieces well. Drain.

Wipe out the pan and add remaining oil. Sauté onion, garlic, and bay leaf for 3 minutes. Add almonds and pine nuts and cook for another minute or till golden. Remove from heat. Remove bay leaf. Keep oil in pan but transfer everything else to a food processor and process to a paste.

In the sauté pan, combine chicken pieces, paste mixture, the oil (left in the pan), saffron, and wine. Add enough water to just barely cover the contents. Season with salt and pepper. Bring to a boil and then reduce heat; simmer over low for about 40 minutes. Serve garnished with chopped hard-boiled egg and with steamed potatoes on the side.

[seville olives]

Peel garlic and pound lightly with a mallet. (You can also lightly pound the olives, but don't mash them.)

Combine olives and garlic in a large bowl with all the herbs and spices as well as the anchovies. Mix well, then pour everything into a jar large enough so the olives fit easily. Add vinegar, add enough water to just cover the contents, close the jar, and shake well.

Marinate at room temperature for 1 week, then refrigerate.

The olives should keep for a long time. They are best when served at room temperature.

Makes about 3 cups
Prep time: 30 minutes
Marinating time: At least 1 week

1 jar (about 2 cups) large Spanish
green olives (gourmet type)
4 cloves garlic
½ teaspoon cumin
2 level teaspoons dried oregano
½ teaspoon fennel seeds
1 small sprig fresh rosemary
1 sprig fresh thyme
1 teaspoon dried thyme
2 bay leaves
2 teaspoons hot *pimentón* or chili
powder (or 1/8 teaspoon cayenne)
4 unsalted anchovy fillets
¼ cup white wine vinegar or
sherry vinegar

Serves 4
Prep time: 10 minutes
Cooking time: 20 minutes

6 cloves garlic
6 small, very firm eggplant
1 small red bell pepper
3 tablespoons olive oil
1–3 tablespoons
sherry vinegar
Mild chili powder
Oregano
Salt and freshly ground
black pepper

[marinated eggplant]

Peel garlic. Rinse eggplant. Cut bell pepper into quarters and remove interiors. In a small frying pan, heat olive oil and lightly brown garlic cloves on all sides over medium heat. Drain.

In a saucepan, bring 1¼ cups water to a boil. Add sautéed garlic, whole eggplants, and bell pepper quarters. Cover and simmer for 5 minutes, then add salt, pepper, a little mild chili powder, and oregano. Then pour in sherry vinegar (more or less, depending on your taste).

Continue simmering uncovered until the eggplant is tender. Keep eggplant in this liquid in a sealed container and refrigerate.

Serve cold.

[fried potatoes with a tomato sauce]

Serves 4–6
Prep time: 30 minutes
Cooking time: About
30 minutes

1 pound smooth-textured
potatoes (e.g., Yukon gold,
fingerlings, red, etc.)
Olive oil for frying or
roasting, plus 3 tablespoons
1 small onion
3 medium ripe tomatoes
1 bay leaf
1 tablespoon tomato paste
1 pinch sugar
1 teaspoon soy sauce
1/2 teaspoon hot *pimentón*
(smoked Spanish paprika;
or substitute chili powder)
1/4 cup dry white wine
1 teaspoon Dijon mustard
Tabasco (optional)
1 tablespoon finely
chopped Italian parsley
Salt and freshly ground
black pepper

There are two ways to prepare the potatoes, either by frying them or by roasting in the oven. In both cases, peel potatoes first, then rinse, dice, and pat dry well. Then fry in a sufficient amount of olive oil (potatoes should brown evenly and not stick together); you'll know the oil is hot enough if you insert a wooden spoon handle down into the oil and lots of tiny bubbles congregate around it. Or, roast by spreading out on a baking sheet, coat well with olive oil, and roast in an oven preheated to 375°F for 20–25 minutes. Make sure they are fully cooked. (If frying potatoes, drain on paper towels.)

While the potatoes are cooking, prepare the sauce. Peel and chop onion. Scald and peel the tomatoes, then mash them. Gently sauté onion along with the bay leaf in 3 tablespoons olive oil until translucent. Add tomato paste, sugar, soy sauce, and *pimentón*. Stir briefly, then add mashed tomatoes and dry white wine. Stir and reduce over medium-high heat. Add Dijon mustard, Tabasco (if using), parsley, salt, and pepper. Keep sauce warm.

Transfer potatoes to a shallow bowl or individual plates, salt, cover with some sauce, and, if desired, several spoonfuls of aïoli (see page 15). Serve immediately.

These *patatas bravas*, one of the most popular tapas, are often served with aïoli (called *allioli* in Spain) but the recipe will be just as delicious if you omit it.

[stuffed chile peppers]

In a saucepan, heat oil and sauté onion and shallot over medium heat for 5 minutes. Add white wine and sherry and reduce liquid by half over medium-high heat. Add fish, bay leaf, parsley, a little salt, and a little water. Cover and simmer over low heat for 10 minutes. Remove fish and mash finely with a fork. Slowly reduce remaining contents of saucepan until nearly all the liquid has evaporated. Then purée in a blender or mash finely. Add pine nuts and currants or raisins, stir, and let cool. Then return fish to this mixture and combine well.

Add black pepper, season with salt to taste, and stir in the beaten egg. Preheat oven to 375°F. Stuff roasted peppers with the fish mixture. Arrange on an ovenproof baking dish, brush with a little olive oil, and roast in the oven for 10 minutes.

Serve hot, warm, or at room temperature.

Serves 4-6
Prep time: 45 minutes
Cooking time: 10 minutes

2 tablespoons olive oil
1 medium chopped onion
1/2 chopped shallot
3/4 cup dry white wine
1/3 cup dry sherry
1/2 pound deboned hake, whiting, or other white fish
1 bay leaf
1 sprig Italian parsley
1 tablespoon pine nuts
1 tablespoon currants or raisins
Salt and freshly ground black pepper
1 beaten egg
12 canned whole roasted red peppers, preferably del piquillo

[meatballs and tomato sauce]

Mix together ground meats, garlic, half the parsley (finely chopped), bread crumbs, and eggs. Season with salt, pepper, and a little *pimentón*. Refrigerate.

Chop tomatoes. Sauté onion in a little of the oil over low heat for 15 minutes. Add sherry, tomatoes, and bay leaf. Add a little water, cover, and simmer gently for 30 minutes.

In the meantime, shape meat mixture into about 20 balls. Heat remaining oil over medium heat and brown the meatballs.

Add salt and pepper to tomato sauce and some *pimentón* to taste. Simmer meatballs in the sauce over low heat for 30 minutes. Serve garnished with remaining parsley.

Serves 4–6
Prep time: 30 minutes
Cooking time: 40 minutes

1/2 pound ground beef
1/2 pound finely ground sausage
3 cloves garlic, grated
1 cup fresh Italian parsley sprigs
3 heaping tablespoons bread crumbs
2 eggs
Sweet *pimentón* (smoked Spanish paprika)
2 pounds tomatoes (scalded and peeled)
1 large chopped onion
1/3 cup olive oil
1/4 cup sherry, preferably *fino*
1 bay leaf
Fresh cilantro (optional)
Salt and freshly ground black pepper

[andalusian gazpacho]

Serves 6–8
Prep time: 35 minutes
Refrigeration time:
At least 2 hours

2 pounds very
ripe tomatoes
2 cloves fresh garlic
1 slice stale French or
Italian bread, without
the crust
1 pinch cumin
2 pinches sweet *pimentón*
(smoked Spanish paprika)
1/3 cup extra virgin olive oil
1/4 cup vinegar (wine or
sherry type)
Salt

For garnish:
1/4 pound green bell pepper
1/4 pound cucumber
1 sweet onion
2 small ripe tomatoes
2 large slices
sourdough bread

Submerge tomatoes in boiling water for several seconds, peel, cut in half, and squeeze gently to remove seeds. Mash flesh and set aside. Peel garlic, discarding any green sprouts.

Soak bread in a little water for 10 minutes. In a blender or food processor, combine bread (drained), tomatoes, garlic, cumin, *pimentón*, and a little salt. Purée while gradually adding olive oil in a thin stream. The mixture will thicken and change color as you add the oil. Add vinegar, then a little water to thin the mixture slightly. Pour mixture into a large bowl or pitcher. Add water until you have the consistency desired but be careful, gazpacho should not be too thin. Refrigerate for at least 2 hours.

Prepare garnish: Peel vegetables and chop finely. Toast bread slices and then cut into croutons. Serve gazpacho with a few ice cubes (in hot weather) and serve croutons and vegetables for garnish on the side in individual bowls. You can also serve gazpacho in glasses or teacups without garnish, or simply with a sprinkling of fresh herbs.

It's possible to buy canned *escabèches* (marinated seafood) from Spain (mussels, squid, and other types of seafood). Although the flavor is very different from this homemade version, don't be afraid to try them.

[mussels escabèche]

Scrub mussels, debeard them if necessary, and rinse well (discard any that aren't closed). Pour wine into a stock pot, add mussels, cover, and bring to a gentle boil, shaking stock pot once, until mussels open (usually about 3–5 minutes). Let cool (discard any that don't open). Remove mussels from shells and set aside. Also set aside ¾ cup of strained cooking liquid.

Peel garlic and carrot, then cut the carrots into into fine matchstick strips. In a cast-iron pan, heat olive oil and brown garlic cloves on all sides. Remove and set aside with the mussels. In the pan, now heat thyme, bay leaf, remaining spices, vinegar (more or less, depending on your taste), and the reserved liquid over very low heat. Simmer gently for 5 minutes, let cool for 3 minutes, and then pour over mussels and garlic. Stir in pickles or capers and carrot strips; cover. Refrigerate for 12 hours.

The next day, remove mussels from the refrigerator 30 minutes before serving.

You can use this same recipe to prepare fish fillets (whole fresh sardines, small red mullet, etc.) or peeled shrimp. In this case, poach the fish or shrimp gently in above marinade by simmering over low heat for 5 minutes before refrigerating.

Serves 4–6
Prep time: 40 minutes
Marinating time: 12 hours
Cooking time: 10 minutes

4 cups fairly large mussels
1¼ cups dry white wine
8 large cloves garlic
1 small carrot
⅓ cup olive oil
1 sprig fresh thyme
2 bay leaves
1 pinch oregano
2 whole cloves
½ teaspoon sweet *pimentón* (smoked Spanish paprika)
¼ cup red wine vinegar, plus more as needed
2 pickles, sliced very thinly or 2 tablespoons rinsed capers
Salt and freshly ground black pepper

[spicy roasted pepper salad]

Serves 4
Prep time: 30 minutes
Standing time: 30 minutes
Cooking time: About
50 minutes

4 large red bell peppers
¼ cup beef or chicken broth
4 large cloves garlic
2 tablespoons olive oil
Sweet or hot *pimentón*
(smoked Spanish paprika)
Salt

Preheat oven to 350°F. Place peppers on a metal baking sheet and roast in the oven for 20 minutes. Turn and roast for another 20 minutes. Remove baking sheet from oven and seal tightly with aluminum foil. Let stand for 30 minutes. Meanwhile, heat the broth.

Uncover peppers and pour hot broth into the pan, scraping up any bits; reserve this liquid. Peel peppers and remove seeds and interiors. Cut pepper flesh into squares. Peel garlic and mash cloves in a mortar and pestle, or crush.

Heat olive oil in a frypan and briefly sauté pepper squares and garlic. Season with salt and *pimentón* to taste and cook over low heat for 3 minutes. Add reserved juices and simmer for 3–5 minutes. Serve warm or at room temperature.

These peppers go very well with meat or fish tapas, whether fried or grilled.

[cream of gazpacho]

Serves 4-6
Prep time: 30 minutes

4 slices stale French or
Italian bread, without
the crust
4 peeled garlic cloves
1 pound tomatoes, scalded,
and peeled
1 small green pepper, diced
½ cup olive oil
¼ cup vinegar (wine or
sherry)
3 slices serrano ham cut
into fine strips
2 sliced hard-boiled eggs
Fine salt

Soak bread in water for 15 minutes. Drain and squeeze out liquid. In a blender, combine bread, garlic, tomatoes, and bell pepper. Process into a smooth cream, season with salt, and add olive oil in a thin stream without stopping the blender. Then add vinegar and combine.

Serve in individual ramekins garnished with serrano ham and sliced hard-boiled egg.

This cream is a thick version of gazpacho, eaten as an appetizer or tapa with good rustic French or Italian bread or raw vegetable sticks.

Serves 4:
Prep time: 15 minutes
Cooking time: 15 minutes

2 ounces slightly fatty
chorizo in one piece
6 slices quality bacon or
prosciutto
12 large pitted dates
(*medjool* variety preferably)

[dates stuffed with chorizo]

Cut chorizo into 12 small strips the same length as the dates and ¼ to ½ inch thick depending on the size of the dates. Halve bacon slices crosswise so you'll have 12 strips for wrapping around the dates.

Stuff each date with one chorizo strip, press together, and wrap with one piece bacon. If necessary, pierce each stuffed date with a toothpick to hold it closed.

Place stuffed dates in a sturdy, well-heated pan with the end of the bacon strip on the bottom. Brown several minutes until the bacon has changed color, then turn stuffed dates carefully and brown the other side, then the other two sides. Make sure the chorizo in the middle is cooked through.

Serve hot.

fall

fall

grape harvest
tapas

Fall tapas tend to go well with strong wines such as sherry, malaga, and port.

These wines signal harvest time, the return to family intimacy, and the season

for more elaborate dishes. Great emphasis is placed on cuisine as part of

celebrations, and these autumn tapas become tiny treasures of conviviality.

Serves 6
Prep time: 45 minutes
Cooking time: 30 minutes

2/3 cup raisins
1/2 pound unsalted salt cod
(ask your fishmonger)
without skin or bones, or
other white fish
1 onion
3 tablespoons olive oil
Sweet or hot *pimentón*
(smoked Spanish paprika)
1 pound *empanada* pastry
(see seafood pockets on
page 20) or ready-to-use
puff pastry
1 egg yolk (optional)
Salt

[small salt-cod and raisin turnovers]

Cover raisins with warm water and set aside. Finely chop or shred salt cod. Peel onion and chop finely.

In a pan, heat olive oil and sauté onion over very low heat for 10 minutes. Add salt cod, stirring well until cooked through (just under 2 minutes). Then add drained raisins. Stir to obtain a uniform filling. Season to taste with salt and add a little *pimentón*.

Preheat oven to 325°F. Roll out pastry into a sheet 1/8 inch thick and cut out circles with a diameter of about 4 1/2 inches. Spread the filling on half of each circle, fold over pastry, and seal the edges with a fork to form crescents.

Place turnovers on a baking sheet and bake for 25–30 minutes. If you want, brush with beaten egg to help them brown. Serve hot or warm.

[galician scallops saint jacques]

Serves 6
Prep time: 35 minutes
Cooking time: 8–10
minutes

2 onions, finely chopped
1/4 cup olive oil
1/4 pound serrano ham,
finely chopped
1 1/4 cups dry white wine
1/3 cup white bread crumbs
12 scallops (Saint Jacques
type), cleaned and rinsed
well, with the coral (save 6
scallop shells; ask your
fishmonger)
Chopped Italian parsley
Salt and freshly ground
pepper

Sauté onions in olive oil. Add serrano ham, salt, and pepper; stir briefly. Add white wine, deglaze the pan, and simmer gently for 5 minutes. Add bread crumbs and stir well until the mixture attains a paste-like consistency. Heat oven broiler and position the rack about 6–8 inches below the broiler.

Place 2 scallops with their coral on each shell. Cover with serrano-bread crumb mixture, sprinkle with chopped parsley, and broil for 8–10 minutes. Serve immediately with *cava* (sparkling wine from Catalonia), champagne, or Italian prosecco.

[pearl onions in sherry vinegar]

Serves 4–6
Prep time: 30 minutes
Marinating time: 1 hour
Cooking time: 2 minutes

1/2 pound very small pearl
onions (no more than 3/4
inch in diameter)
2 tablespoons sea salt
1 1/4 cups sherry vinegar
1 spicy red chile pepper
without seeds, crumbled, or
1/2 teaspoon hot *pimentón*
8 black peppercorns
1 bay leaf
1 pinch dried thyme
4 whole cloves

Submerge pearl onions in a saucepan of boiling water, remove from heat, and let stand for 2 minutes. Rinse under cold water and peel. Transfer to a bowl, add sea salt, and cover with 1 cup water. Marinate for 1 hour and then rinse and drain.

In a small saucepan, bring sherry vinegar to a boil. Add onions, chile or *pimentón*, black peppercorns, bay leaf, thyme, and whole cloves. Simmer over low heat for 2 minutes and then remove from heat. Transfer to a container, cover, and refrigerate. Serve cold.

These onions go well with patés, terrines, and charcuterie (sausages, cured meats, and forcemeats).

[mini cheese and chile pepper soufflés]

Generously butter 6 ramekins (set rest of butter aside). Combine 1 tablespoon flour and two-thirds of the walnuts, and coat the bottom of the ramekins with this mixture, shaking them in all directions to cover the sides. Set aside. Preheat oven to 375°F.

Bring milk to a boil, remove from heat, and set aside. Separate eggs. Melt remaining butter in a saucepan. Stir in 6 tablespoons flour and then the chile peppers and cook on medium-low for 3 minutes while stirring with a spatula. Add milk while stirring constantly and beat vigorously with a wire whisk if lumps form. Simmer over low heat for 3 minutes. Remove from heat and let cool slightly, then stir in grated cheese, 1 pinch sea salt, egg yolks, mustard, and a little pepper.

Using an electric mixer, beat egg whites and 1 pinch salt into firm but not rigid peaks. With a rubber spatula, delicately fold one-fourth of the egg whites into the sauce, and then add the rest gently and quickly to obtain a uniform mixture. Spread mixture in the ramekins with a spoon. Sprinkle with remaining chopped walnuts and bake in the oven for 15–25 minutes until the soufflés have risen. Serve immediately.

Serves 6:
Prep time: 1 hour
Cooking time: About
25 minutes

7 tablespoons butter
Flour
1/2 cup chopped walnuts
1 1/2 cups milk
3 large eggs
2 spicy red chile peppers
without seeds and finely
chopped or 2 teaspoons
crushed red pepper flakes
1/4 pound grated Manchego
or Ibérico cheese (may
substitute aged Cheddar
or Parmesan)
1 teaspoon prepared
mustard
Sea salt and freshly
ground pepper

[stuffed calamaris in their own ink]

Serves 4–6
Prep time: 90 minutes
Cooking time: 50 minutes

2 pounds small, very
fresh whole squid (ask
your fishmonger)
1 slice serrano ham
1 shallot
1 hard-boiled egg
⅓ cup olive oil
Flour

For the sauce:
1 large onion
3 cloves garlic
1 fresh green chile pepper
⅓ cup tomato sauce
1 cup fish stock
1¼ cups dry white wine
2 tablespoons brandy
(optional)
Garlic croutons (you can
make your own by frying
bread cubes in olive oil
and then rubbing them
with fresh garlic)
Salt

Clean squid by gently rubbing them under cold water. Empty their interiors but save all the ink sacs without puncturing them. Ask your fishmonger to help clean the squid if necessary. Chop the tentacles along with the serrano ham, shallot, and hard-boiled egg. Stuff the squid tubes or "fillets," but not too full. Close the opening with toothpicks and dredge in flour. In a sturdy pot, sauté lightly in olive oil. Remove and set aside.

Peel garlic and onion and chop both finely. Split open chile pepper, remove seeds, and chop rest finely. In the same oil as the squid, slowly sauté onion, garlic, and green chile pepper until onion is translucent. Add tomato sauce and stir.

In a mixing bowl, puncture ink sacs and dilute with fish stock. Return squid to the stock pot and add diluted ink, white wine, and brandy (if using). Season with salt, bring to a boil, cover, and simmer over very low heat for 45 minutes. Serve with fried garlic croutons.

You can serve these little squid alone as a tapa or with rice.

[bell peppers cadiz style]

Serves 4–6
Prep time: 30 minutes
Refrigeration time: At least
1 hour

2 red bell peppers and 2
green bell peppers, roasted
and peeled (see page 48)
1 large ripe tomato
1 onion
2 tablespoons olive oil
1 tablespoon wine vinegar
or sherry vinegar
Salt and freshly ground
black pepper

Finely chop peppers. Submerge tomatoes in boiling water for several seconds and remove peel. Squeeze out seeds and chop rest finely. Peel and finely chop onion.

Mix all ingredients together in a large earthenware bowl and refrigerate for at least 1 hour before serving.

These peppers can be served as a salad but also go well with all sorts of hot dishes, especially grilled and roasted meats, skewers, and grilled or fried fish.

[cheese fritters]

Beat egg whites into firm peaks. Using a rubber spatula, gently fold in grated cheese, *pimentón*, and 3 teaspoons of the flour.

Heat oil. Cover your hands with remaining flour and shape cheese-egg mixture into balls, placing one cube of ham inside each one. Brown in the olive oil and serve immediately.

These small fritters are especially delicious with an aperitif of dry sherry. They are great served with cornichons or other pickles.

Serves 4
Prep time: 25 minutes
Cooking time: About
3 minutes

2 egg whites
5 ounces grated cheese
(Manchego, ewe's or goat's
milk cheese, Cheddar, etc.)
1 pinch hot *pimentón*
(smoked Spanish paprika)
4 teaspoons flour
1 thick slice serrano or other
ham, cut into small cubes
Olive oil

Serves 4
Prep time: 40 minutes
Cooking time: 45 minutes

1 pound spareribs from
young pork (the bones
should be somewhat fine;
ask your butcher)
3 tablespoons olive oil
1¼ cups chicken stock
and/or dry white wine
1 bay leaf
2 cloves garlic
3 sprigs Italian parsley,
finely chopped
1 teaspoon hot *pimentón* or
1 spicy red chile pepper
without seeds, finely
crumbled
Salt

[pork spareribs in garlic sauce]

With a sharp knife, cut apart ribs between the bones so as to obtain small strips containing meat. Then cut these strips into pieces 1½ inch thick, using a cleaver to cut through the bones.

Heat olive oil and brown pork ribs well. Add stock or dry white wine and bay leaf. Season with salt, cover, and simmer over low heat for 45 minutes. Skim any visible fat from the surface.

Finely crush garlic and mix with parsley, a little salt, and the *pimentón* or chile pepper.

Remove pork spareribs from heat and just before serving, add this paste. Stir, cover, and let stand for 2 minutes. Serve with rustic bread.

[monkfish packets]

Serves 4–6
Prep time: 90 minutes
Cooking time: 10 minutes

1 small carrot
½ cup sugar snap peas
1 cup vegetable stock
(prepared with water, carrot,
leek, celery, bay leaves,
thyme, parsley, salt and
pepper, boiled for 40
minutes)
1 large green onion
2 tablespoons melted butter
½ cup crème fraîche
½ pound monkfish or other
firm white fish, deboned and
cut into as many pieces as
there are guests
Salt and freshly ground
white pepper

Preheat oven to 375°F. Peel carrot and cut into fine matchstick strips. Rinse sugar snap peas, trim away ends, and cut lengthwise into strips. Place carrot and pea strips in a saucepan, pour in vegetable stock, and bring to a boil. Cover and simmer for 3 minutes. Drain, saving the stock.

Cut green onion into julienne strips, then sauté lightly in melted butter. Remove cooked green onion and set aside. Add reserved vegetable stock and crème fraîche to butter and reduce by two thirds over medium heat. Salt to taste and add pepper. Prepare as many sheets of aluminum foil (or baking parchment) as there are guests. Place a piece of monkfish on each sheet, season with salt and pepper, and add julienned vegetables and stewed green onions.

Distribute sauce evenly over the packet contents, seal them tight, and bake for 10 minutes. Let guests open their packets at the table.

[manchego with quince paste]

Serves 4–6
Prep time: 15 minutes

½ pound manchego,
fromage des Pyrènèes, or
ewe's milk Tomme cheese
½ pound quince paste (the
type that is sliced or can
be sliced)

Cut cheese into even slices and then into squares or rectangles. Cut quince paste into slices of the same shape, size, and thickness and place on top of cheese slices.

Then cut all slices into triangles (or leave in squares) and even up the edges. Serve with a toothpick pierced through the stack.

Serve with *fino* or *amontillado* sherry. You can also try this tapa with a sweet wine (e.g., port, malaga, muscat, etc.).

The sweet and earthy flavor of the humble beet is elevated here by the spicy aroma of anise seed—a divine recipe for cooked beets. If using leftover cooked beets, just extend the marinating time by several hours.

[beet and anise seed salad]

Remove beet tops and scrub beets well under running water. Place in a saucepan, add enough water to cover beets, and bring to a boil. Add a little salt, cover, and simmer 40 minutes to 1 hour, depending on the size of the beets, until you can easily pierce them with the tip of a knife. Drain beets, let cool, peel, and slice as desired. Set aside.

Crush anise seed slightly in a mortar and pestle. Peel and finely chop shallot or onion. Place anise seed in a small bowl with olive oil, sherry vinegar, a little salt, and the *pimentón*. Whisk well and then stir in shallot. Season beets with this vinaigrette. Refrigerate until ready to serve.

This salad is even better after marinating for 1–2 days.

Serves 4–6
Prep time: 30 minutes
Cooking time: 1 hour

1 pound small raw beets
½ teaspoon anise seeds
1 shallot or 1 small onion
⅓ cup extra virgin olive oil
3 tablespoons
sherry vinegar
Salt
Sweet or hot *pimentón*
(smoked Spanish paprika)

[crispy fish fillets]

Serves 6
Prep time: 35 minutes
Cooking time: 4 minutes

6 thin, very fresh fish fillets
(e.g., sole, hake)
Juice of 1 lemon
$\frac{1}{2}$ pound small squid fillets
and tentacles
$\frac{1}{2}$ pound marinated
anchovy fillets (page 29) or
fresh anchovy fillets
6 small striped red mullets
(whole small fish)
6 large or 12 medium
shrimp
$\frac{3}{4}$ cup flour
$\frac{1}{4}$ cup sparkling water
Olive oil for pan frying or
deep frying
Lemons
Salt

Rinse fish fillets and pat dry. Salt on both sides, drizzle with a little lemon juice, and set aside. Rinse squid and pat dry. Pat dry anchovy fillets. Scale red mullets, pat dry, and clean without removing liver (located behind the head); or, ask your fishmonger to do this for you. Dry red mullets well with paper towels and set aside. Peel shrimp, except for the tails, and de-vein with the tip of a knife. Salt lightly. Set aside all fish and heat olive oil (at least $\frac{1}{2}$ inch in the bottom of a sauté pan if pan frying or a larger quantity in a pot for deep frying).

Combine half of the flour with the sparkling water and a little salt to form a somewhat liquidy batter. Put the rest of the flour on a plate for dredging. As for the oil, you'll be able to tell when it's ready by this: lower the handle of a wooden spoon into the oil—if it's time, lots of tiny bubbles will congregate around it.

Work very fast. Lightly salt red mullets, squid pieces, and anchovy fillets and dredge each in flour, shaking off excess. Pat dry fish fillets and dredge in flour. Dip shrimp in batter while holding them by the tail.

Immediately after dredging fish in flour and dipping shrimp in batter, brown on all sides in hot oil, either for about 2 minutes on each side or by immersing for 3–4 minutes if deep-frying. Drain briefly on paper towels.

Serve very hot with lemon wedges. The flavor of this recipe depends not only on the freshness of the fish and how they are cooked (they should not be too done) but also on the quality of the olive oil.

[grilled tuna with marinated tomatoes]

Peel garlic and chop finely. Combine 3 tablespoons olive oil, garlic, chopped parsley, grated citrus zest, a little salt and pepper, and lemon or mandarin orange juice. Place tuna in this marinade and turn and marinate for about 2 hours at room temperature.

Submerge tomatoes in boiling water, peel, remove seeds, and mash the tomato flesh. Place in a shallow bowl. Combine vinegar, 3 tablespoons olive oil, sugar, salt, and pepper; season tomatoes with this mixture. Set aside.

Cook tuna steak in the oven under the broiler, on the barbecue, or sear in a pan with a little olive oil. Cook for about 2 minutes on each side. It should be well-seared but still pink in the middle. Cut into 4–6 pieces and serve on top of the marinated tomatoes.

Serves 6
Prep time: 30 minutes
Marinating time: 2 hours
Cooking time: 4 minutes

1 large clove garlic
Olive oil
1 tablespoon chopped Italian parsley
1 teaspoon finely grated lemon or mandarin orange zest
2 teaspoons lemon or mandarin orange juice
1 thick fresh tuna steak (about a pound, rinsed and patted dry)
4 large ripe tomatoes
1 teaspoon white wine vinegar
1 pinch sugar
Sea salt and freshly ground black pepper

Scrub mussels, debeard if necessary, and rinse. Throw away any mussels that don't close during this process. In a saucepan, heat olive oil and lightly sauté green onions. Add flour and simmer for another minute while stirring well, gradually adding wine, then mustard, and then salt and pepper. Rinse and finely chop chervil and add last of all. Cover and simmer for 3 minutes over low heat.

Add mussels, cover saucepan, and simmer for about 4–5 minutes or until most of the mussels open. Throw away any mussels that still remain closed. Drizzle with lemon juice, distribute on plates or in individual ramekins, and serve while hot.

Serves 6–8
Prep time: 35 minutes
Cooking time: 10–12 minutes

4 cups mussels
2 tablespoons olive oil
2 chopped green onions
1 teaspoon flour
$1/2$ cup dry white wine
1 teaspoon mustard
$3/4$ cup fresh chervil sprigs
Juice of $1/2$ lemon
Salt and freshly ground
white pepper

[chervil mussels]

The wines of Jerez are first aged in casks, where a yeast

called *flor* gives the sherry its distinctive flavor. Later, the

sherry is transferred to the *solera*, a system of stacked

rows of oak casks through which it is processed by

rotation. Wine from the bottom row is bottled while the top

row is refilled with "new" wine. The best sherries (or "jerez")

have the date of the creation of their *solera* on the label.

[savory chicken liver flan]

Serves 6
Prep time: 1 hour
Cooking time: 35 minutes

1 small onion
½ pound chicken livers,
trimmed and de-veined
1 tablespoon butter
2 eggs
¾ cup + 2 tablespoons
half-and-half
3 tablespoons *oloroso*
sherry (medium sweet)
½ teaspoon hot or sweet
pimentón (smoked
Spanish paprika)
1 large pinch grated nutmeg
1 tablespoon finely
chopped Italian parsley
¼ cup sugar
Salt and freshly ground
black pepper

Preheat oven to 325°F. Place a large roasting pan containing 1 inch of simmering water on the bottom into the oven. Peel and finely chop onion. Cut chicken livers in half and sauté in butter with chopped onion until seared but still pink in the middle. In a blender, process into a fine paste. **I**n a bowl, beat eggs, half-and-half, 1 tablespoon of the sherry, salt, and pepper. Add *pimentón*, nutmeg, and chopped parsley. Add this mixture to the contents of blender and mix well.

Butter 6 ramekins, fill with the mixture, and lower ramekins down into the water in the roasting pan (water should come partway up the ramekin sides). Bake for about 35 minutes.

Prepare the sauce: To a small saucepan add the sugar and 2 teaspoons water. Simmer over low heat while stirring to obtain a caramel. As soon as it turns brown, add half the remaining sherry, stir well, and remove from heat. Add remaining sherry and 2 teaspoons water; stir.

Before serving, reverse ramekins onto small individual plates and top flans with the sherry caramel. Serve while hot.

Serves 4–6
Prep time: 45 minutes
Cooking time: 5 minutes

4 large potatoes
A little hot milk
1 egg, separated
2 tablespoons flour
Olive oil for pan-frying

For the cheese balls:
1/2 teaspoon baking powder
1/4 cup grated cheese
1 tablespoon finely
chopped onion
Grated nutmeg
1 tablespoon finely
chopped Italian parsley
Salt and freshly ground
black pepper

For the meatballs:
1/4 cup sautéed ground meat
1 tablespoon finely
chopped Italian parsley
Salt and freshly ground
black pepper

[fried potato balls]

Rinse potatoes and boil for about 25 minutes or until easily pierced with the tip of a knife. Peel and mash with a little hot milk, the egg yolk, and the flour to form a dense yet smooth purée. Divide in half and set aside. Beat egg white and set aside.

Cheese balls: Combine one-half of the potato purée with the baking powder, grated cheese, onion, nutmeg, parsley, salt, and pepper. Shape into balls and set aside.

Meatballs: Mix ground meat with parsley, salt, and pepper. Shape into balls, then flatten each one in the palm of your hand, add a little of the potato filling to the center, and reshape the ball around it.

In a cast-iron pan, heat a good amount of olive oil for pan-frying. Dip both types of balls in beaten egg white and then fry immediately on all sides. Remove when browned.

Serve while hot.

winter

winter

tapas that warm you up

The cold season brings with it more substantial tapas, those simmered dishes and earthy foods that can only come from Spanish soil. Winter products— including wild mushrooms, chestnuts, cured meats, and legumes—are very well suited to creating an array of tapas. Also, there is nothing more comforting in cold weather than a feast of small plates enjoyed with rioja or dry sherry.

Serves 6–8
Prep time: 10 minutes
Standing time: 11 hours
Cooking time: About
25 minutes

2 uncooked Spanish
chorizo sausages (total
of ½ pound)
2 cups dry white wine or
fino sherry (dry)

[chorizo marinated in white wine]

Pierce chorizos with a fork and place in a small saucepan. Add half the wine, bring to a boil, cover, and simmer for 20 minutes. Let stand one hour at room temperature, then refrigerate the chorizo, still soaking in the wine, for another 10 hours.

The next day, drain and slice the chorizos and place the pieces in a small pan. Add remaining wine and reduce over high heat. Serve hot.

You can also add a little dry sherry to the marinating wine or use sherry alone.

[fillet of sole with pine nuts and raisins]

Serves 6
Prep time: 30 minutes
Cooking time: 15 minutes

6 sole fillets
2 tablespoons olive oil
2 tablespoons white
bread crumbs
2 tablespoons crushed
pine nuts
2 tablespoons raisins
or currants
2 tablespoons grated
Parmesan or manchego
2 tablespoons finely
chopped Italian parsley
Juice of 1 lemon
1 cup dry white wine
Salt and freshly ground
black pepper

Preheat oven to 350°F. Season fish fillets with salt and pepper and brush with olive oil. Set aside.

Combine bread crumbs, pine nuts, raisins or currants, Parmesan or manchego, and parsley; generously sprinkle on fish fillets (reserving a little for later). Roll up fillets, secure with toothpicks, and place in a greased baking dish with sides. Add white wine and drizzle everything with some olive oil and the fresh lemon juice. Sprinkle with remaining bread crumb mixture and bake for 15 minutes.

Serve hot, warm, or room temperature, but not chilled.

[carrot salad with cumin]

Serves 4–6
Prep time: 35 minutes
Marinating time: 12 hours
Cooking time: 20 minutes

1 pound baby carrots
2 large cloves garlic
2 tablespoons
sherry vinegar
¼ cup olive oil
1 teaspoon hot *pimentón*
(smoked Spanish paprika)
1 teaspoon cumin
1 pinch dried oregano
Salt

Peel carrots. Submerge whole carrots in a saucepan of boiling salted water (don't use too much water; it should barely cover the carrots) and simmer for 20 minutes over low heat. Drain.

Peel garlic cloves and grate finely. For the dressing, combine the following in a large bowl: garlic, sherry vinegar, olive oil, *pimentón*, cumin, and oregano. Season with salt. Slice carrots and add to dressing. Stir well, cover, and marinate overnight in the refrigerator.

This salad goes very well with grilled meat tapas (such as the marinated skewers on page 81) or any grilled seafood such as tuna. Serve chilled or, even better, at room temperature.

[meatballs in an almond-saffron sauce]

Moisten bread crumbs with several spoonfuls of the wine. Grate 3 of the garlic cloves. Combine grated garlic, bread crumbs, the ground meats, eggs, half the chopped parsley, salt, and pepper; mix well. Shape into balls the size of small walnuts.

In a saucepan, heat olive oil and quickly brown meatballs, stirring occasionally. Remove and set aside, keeping them warm (they will cook more later). In the same saucepan, sauté the onion and carrot. Add remaining wine and remaining garlic cloves. Reduce over medium heat until almost all the liquid has evaporated. Remove from heat.

In a food processor, reduce almonds to a very fine powder. Gradually add stock while continuing to run food processor. Pour this mixture into the saucepan, add meatballs, remaining parsley, saffron, and bay leaf. Season to taste. Cover and return to heat, simmering for 45 minutes. Serve hot, sprinkled with snipped chives.

Serves 6–8
Prep time: 1 hour
Cooking time: About 1 hour

1/2 cup bread crumbs
1 2/3 cups dry white wine
14 peeled garlic cloves
1/2 pound ground beef
1/3 pound ground veal
1 pound ground pork
2 beaten eggs
1/2 cup fresh Italian parsley sprigs, finely chopped
2 tablespoons olive oil
1 finely chopped medium onion
1 small finely grated carrot
25 skinless blanched almonds
2 cups chicken or beef stock
1 pinch saffron threads, toasted briefly in a dry pan and then crumbled
1 bay leaf
8 fresh chive spears
Sea salt and freshly ground pepper

[dried fruit marmalade]

Prep time: 15 minutes
Soaking time: 1 hour
Cooking time: 20 minutes

1 medium onion
1 small orange
2 tablespoons raisins
2 tablespoons pitted prunes
1 finely chopped shallot
1/3 cup *amontillado* sherry
(medium dry sherry)
1 teaspoon finely grated
lemon zest
Juice of 1/2 lemon
1/3 cup red currant jelly
1 teaspoon peppercorns
2 tablespoons coarsely
crushed pine nuts
1 tablespoon
slivered almonds
1/2 teaspoon
prepared mustard
Fine salt

Peel onion, cut into quarters, and soak for 1 hour in a bowl of very salty water. Zest orange. Squeeze juice from orange. With a knife, coarsely chop raisins and prunes and mix with orange zest. Place in a small saucepan along with shallot, orange juice, sherry, grated lemon zest, and fresh lemon juice. Simmer, uncovered, over low heat for 20 minutes. Let cool.

Drain onion and chop finely. Combine contents of saucepan with onion, red currant jelly, peppercorns, pine nuts, almonds, and mustard. Serve with terrines or pâtés and bread.

Keep this sauce in the refrigerator in a screw-top jar.

[castilian-style garlic soup]

Serves 6–8
Prep time: 25 minutes
Cooking time: 10 minutes

1 head of garlic
1/4 cup olive oil
4 ounces diced serrano ham
4 slices stale rustic French
or Italian bread, cut into
cubes
1 teaspoon sweet *pimentón*
(smoked Spanish paprika)
4 cups chicken stock
6 eggs

Peel and slice garlic cloves but not too thinly. In a pot, heat oil and lightly brown garlic over medium heat. Add diced serrano ham and bread and let brown for several minutes. Add *pimentón* and stock. Salt to taste and bring to a boil. Reduce heat and simmer gently for 5 minutes, then break eggs one by one into the stock mixture to poach them. Simmer over very low heat for 3 minutes.

Remove eggs with a slotted spoon and distribute them in small bowls. Pour garlic soup over the top and serve while hot.

[tuna "meatballs" in white wine]

Chop fish very finely. In a bowl, moisten bread crumbs with a little stock and 1 tablespoon of the wine. Add chopped tuna, beaten egg, chopped hard-boiled egg, chopped parsley, salt, and pepper. Mix well and form into small balls.

In a pan, heat oil. Dredge tuna balls in flour and fry in pan, turning so they brown well. Add remaining wine and all the stock plus a little salt. Cover and simmer over low heat for 30 minutes. If the mixture dries out too much, add a little stock. Serve hot, warm, or at room temperature.

Serves 4–6
Prep time: 40 minutes
Cooking time: 30 minutes

½ pound fresh albacore tuna
⅓ cup white bread crumbs
1 cup chicken stock
1 cup dry white wine
1 beaten egg
1 finely chopped hard-boiled egg
3 tablespoons finely chopped Italian parsley
2 large cloves garlic, finely chopped
3 tablespoons olive oil
Flour
Salt and freshly ground black pepper

Serves 6
Prep time: 30 minutes
Cooking time: 6–12 minutes
Marinating time: 12 hours

1 pound pork or lamb
1 small onion
2 cloves garlic
1 tablespoon Italian parsley
1 teaspoon *pimentón*
(smoked Spanish paprika)
3 tablespoons olive oil
Several saffron threads,
toasted briefly in a dry pan
1 pinch dried oregano
½ teaspoon cumin
Salt and freshly ground
black pepper

[marinated pork skewers]

Remove any sinews from meat with a sharp knife, then cut into 1-inch cubes. Peel garlic and chop finely. Thinly slice onion. Finely chop parsley. In a large bowl, combine these with all the other ingredients and add meat cubes. Stir well, cover, and refrigerate for 12 hours.

The next day, remove meat from the refrigerator 1 hour before serving. Also, soak some bamboo skewers in water (so they don't burn later). Thread meat cubes onto bamboo skewers (3–4 pieces per skewer).

Preheat oven broiler for 5 minutes and broil skewers while intermittently brushing with marinade. If lamb, cook for 3 minutes on each side and if pork, for 5–6 minutes on each side. Sprinkle with salt. Serve hot.

[garbanzo beans in onion sauce]

Place garbanzo beans in a bowl of warm water with a pinch of baking soda and soak for 12 hours.

The next day, drain garbanzos. Peel onions and garlic. Cover beans with fresh water, add small onion, whole garlic clove, and bay leaf; bring to a boil.

Cover and simmer for about 1½ hours until the garbanzos are tender. Salt when done, drain, and remove onion, garlic, and bay leaf.

Thinly slice the large onion. Submerge tomato in boiling water for 30 seconds, peel, and mash flesh. In a sauté pan, heat olive oil and sauté the slices from the large onion for 1 minute. Add tomato, cover, and simmer over very low heat for 10 minutes. The onion should be cooked without browning. Now add garbanzos, stir, and serve hot or warm.

Serves 4–6
Prep time: 30 minutes
Soaking time: 12 hours
Cooking time: 1 hour
45 minutes

1¼ cups dried
garbanzo beans
1 pinch baking soda
2 onions (1 small and
1 large)
1 clove garlic
1 bay leaf
2 tablespoons olive oil
1 medium tomato
Salt

For this recipe to succeed, the octopus must be well tenderized (as specified below) and cooked for a fairly long time. In addition, the potatoes should be served warm (if using). Enjoy with a white Rueda wine, a very fruity *rias baixas*, a *valdeorras,* or any other Spanish white wine.

[galician-style octopus]

Have your fishmonger clean the octopus for you. Tenderize it: Some people pound it for a long time with a mallet while others throw it down hard into the sink ten or twenty times. But you can also freeze it for 12 hours and then thaw it for 6 hours in the refrigerator (this is the longest but easiest solution).

In a stockpot, bring a large amount of water to a boil with all the ingredients listed for the vegetable stock. Grasp the octopus with tongs, submerge it in the boiling stock for several seconds, and then remove it. Drain several seconds and then submerge for a second time and remove as before. Repeat this procedure a third time, then place octopus in the stock, cover, and simmer for about 1 hour. Test whether it's done by tasting a small piece. If it's still rubbery, continue cooking. When it's done cooking, remove from heat and let octopus cool in the cooking liquid until serving.

In the meantime, boil the potatoes (if using) until they can be easily pierced with a paring knife (usually about 20–25 minutes). Peel, slice, and place on a large platter. Drain octopus and cut into pieces. Arrange pieces on top of the potatoes, drizzle with olive oil, and sprinkle with *pimentón* and sea salt. Serve immediately.

Serves 6–8
Prep time: 40 minutes
Freezing and thawing time:
18 hours
Cooking time: about
75 minutes

2 pounds octopus (ask your fishmonger; pre-order if necessary)
Potatoes (optional)
1/4 cup very fruity olive oil
1/2 teaspoon sweet or hot *pimentón* (smoked Spanish paprika)
1 tablespoon sea salt

For the vegetable stock:
1 handful kosher or other coarse salt
2 tablespoons olive oil
1 bay leaf
1 whole, peeled onion (or shallot)
1 teaspoon black peppercorns
2 sprigs Italian parsley
1/2 spicy fresh or dried red chile pepper (without seeds)

[mandarin orange monkfish]

Serves 4–6
Prep time: 35 minutes
Cooking time: 15 minutes

1 pound monkfish (or any
other firm white fish)
2 tablespoons fresh
lime juice
1 tablespoon olive oil
3 thinly sliced green onions
1 tablespoon Italian parsley
1¼ cups dry white wine
1 scant cup mandarin
orange juice
7 tablespoons very cold
butter in one piece
Salt and freshly ground
white pepper

If necessary, remove backbone from tail end of fish (or have fishmonger do this). Cut fish into cubes of about 1½ to 2 inches. Season with a little salt and pepper, drizzle with lime juice, and let stand for 15 minutes.

Preheat oven to 375°F.

Grease a roasting pan. Place fish pieces in the pan with juice. Pour olive oil over the top. Sprinkle with sliced green onions and chopped Italian parsley. Finally, pour in the wine and mandarin orange juice and bake for 10 minutes. Make sure fish pieces are cooked through. Remove the cooking juices and cook over high heat in a saucepan to reduce to one-third of the original volume. Cover fish in baking pan with foil to keep warm. Then remove cooking juices from heat and add butter. Swirl the pan around to melt the butter and thicken the sauce.

Pour this sauce over the fish and serve immediately. You can serve this fancy tapa with a little saffron rice.

[mushrooms stuffed with serrano ham]

Preheat oven to 350°F. Peel and finely chop garlic. Combine serrano ham, garlic, parsley, *pimentón*, and olive oil; mix well. Fill mushroom caps with this mixture and place in an ovenproof dish. Bake for 15 minutes.

Serve hot, warm, or cold.

Serves 4
Prep time: 25 minutes
Cooking time: 15 minutes

12 open mushroom caps
with a 4-inch diameter
(portobella recommended)
2 large cloves garlic
3 tablespoons finely diced
serrano ham
2 tablespoons finely
chopped Italian parsley
½ teaspoon hot *pimentón*
(smoked Spanish paprika)
1 tablespoon very fruity
olive oil

[garbanzo bean salad]

Serves 6–8
Prep time: 30 minutes
Refrigeration time: 4 hours

In a large bowl, mix garbanzos, diced tomato, hard-boiled eggs, parsley, anchovies (if using), and olives.

For the vinaigrette, mix together the olive oil, sherry vinegar, a little salt, and the *pimentón*. Add to garbanzos and toss. Refrigerate for several hours.

Remove salad from the refrigerator 30 minutes before serving. If the garbanzos seem a little dry, add oil and taste. You can also add a little more vinegar if desired.

Also, note that navy beans can be used in place of the garbanzo beans in this recipe.

1 pound cooked garbanzo
beans (canned are acceptable)
1 peeled, diced tomato
2 hard-boiled eggs (peeled,
halved lengthwise, and sliced)
1 tablespoon chopped Italian
parsley
4 anchovy fillets packed in oil
(optional), cut into quarters
6 pitted black kalamata
olives, quartered
3 tablespoons very fruity
olive oil
1 tablespoon sherry vinegar
1 large clove garlic, grated
Salt
Hot *pimentón* (smoked
Spanish paprika)

Using a fork, mash the cheese to make it into a paste. Peel the pears, cut in half, and remove cores. Drizzle pear halves with lemon juice so they don't turn brown. Set aside. Heat olive oil for frying and fry sage leaves for about 20 seconds. Drain on paper towels and salt lightly.

Just before serving, cut pear halves in half again and top each piece with 1 teaspoon of the mashed blue cheese. Top with a sage leaf, pierce with a toothpick, and serve.

This refined tapa goes best with a good dry sherry or *oloroso*.

Serves 4–6
Prep time: 20 minutes

$\frac{1}{3}$ to $\frac{1}{2}$ pound very ripe Cabrales (Spanish blue) or any other blue cheese
3 large pears (cornice or Williams), ripe but firm
Juice of $\frac{1}{2}$ lemon
18–20 fresh sage leaves
Olive oil for frying
Salt

[pears with blue cheese and sage]

Manchego is Spain's most famous cheese. Made from ewe's milk,

it is both rich and tender. But you should also try some others,

including: Cabrales, a blue from Asturias; Tetilla, a delicate

Galician cheese whose name (meaning "breast") aptly describes

its shape; Majón from Minorca, rubbed with paprika; Majorero,

a goat cheese from the Canary Islands; and Zamorano, a cooked-

paste cheese from Castille-Leon made from ewe's milk.

[potatoes with cheese and chile peppers]

Serves 6–8
Prep time: 35 minutes
Cooking time: 30 minutes

1 spicy dried red chile
pepper without seeds,
crumbled
1 onion
¼ cup fresh lemon juice
1 pinch hot *pimentón*
(smoked Spanish paprika)
8 medium potatoes (any
type)
1 pound mild Cheddar or
manchego (i.e., semi-hard
cheese), cubed or grated
1 teaspoon sweet *pimentón*
⅔ cup crème fraîche
¼ cup olive oil
4 hard-boiled eggs
Lettuce leaves
Black kalamata olives, pitted
Salt and pepper

Soak crumbled chile pepper in a little warm water for 30 minutes. Peel onion, slice thinly, and marinate in fresh lemon juice along with salt, pepper, and hot *pimentón*. Boil potatoes until they pierce easily with a knife tip (usually about 20–25 minutes), peel, and keep warm.

In a blender, combine cheese, spicy red chile pepper (drained), sweet *pimentón,* and crème fraîche; reduce to a paste. In a pan, heat olive oil and pour in this mixture. Simmer over low heat while stirring constantly with a wooden spatula until you have a smooth and creamy sauce.

Arrange lettuce leaves on a platter. Cut potatoes into thick slices and arrange them on the lettuce. Cover with cheese sauce. Garnish with sliced hard-boiled eggs, pitted olives, and marinated onion slices.

This recipe from Peru fits in perfectly with a tapas buffet. It's important that you serve it warm or hot, but never cold.

[quail "a la plancha"]

Serves 4
Prep time: 30 minutes
Marinating time: 12 hours
Cooking time: 7–8 minutes

6 cloves garlic, crushed
1 small onion, thinly sliced
¼ cup dry white wine
1 teaspoon red wine vinegar
3 tablespoons olive oil
1 pinch dried thyme
4 quail, halved lengthwise
Salt

"**A** la Plancha" means "grilled or broiled." For making this tapa, combine garlic, onion, wine, vinegar, salt, and oil in a mortar, blender, or food processor; process to a paste. Add thyme. Pour this paste into a shallow bowl. Coat the quail in this marinade and let sit with the skin side down. Cover and refrigerate for 12 hours.

The next day, remove quail from refrigerator 1 hour before serving. Preheat oven broiler and place quail on a metal cooking sheet with the skin side down (lift it out of the marinade first, but reserve the marinade). Slide under the broiler and broil quail for 3 minutes. Turn, brush with marinade, and broil for another minute. Turn once more, brush with more marinade, and broil for 1 more minute. Turn quail one more time and with the skin side up, brush with remaining marinade, and brown under the broiler for about 2 minutes. Alternatively, you can grill the quail halves and, in a similar way, brush with marinade and turn periodically. Make sure quail is cooked through—should be opaque. Serve hot.

desserts & beverages

desserts & beverages

almonds and citrus fruits

There's a touch of the Middle East in Spanish desserts, retained from the influence of ancient Muslim Andalusia. These desserts contain the same precious ingredients found in Moroccan baked goods, such as almonds, oranges, lemons, orange blossom water, and spices (cinnamon and green anise). These creamy, caramelized, aromatic, sweet desserts add a sophisticated finishing touch to a meal of colorful, flavorful tapas.

Serves 4:
Prep time: 30 minutes
Refrigeration time: At least
1 hour

1/2 cup sugar
8 egg yolks
Grated zest of 1 lemon
A little almond extract

[lemon cream]

Preheat oven to 300°F. Place a large ovenproof baking dish (containing 1 1/2 inches of near-boiling water in the bottom) into the oven.

Pour 1/2 cup water into a saucepan, add sugar, and melt over low heat until you have a thick syrup.

Whisk egg yolks while adding sugar syrup in a thin stream. Fold in lemon peel.

Rub 4 ramekins with a little almond extract, pour in lemon cream, and lower them down into the prepared pan in the oven (the hot water should come partway up the sides of the ramekins).

Cover the whole pan with a sheet of aluminum foil and bake for 20–25 minutes. The cream should be firm to the touch. Let cool for one hour, covered with aluminum foil, and then refrigerate until serving.

[almond horchata]

Serves 6
Prep time: 35 minutes
Standing time: 2 hours
Refrigeration time: At least
2 hours

1 pound blanched
skinless almonds
1 pinch salt
1 lemon, sliced
1 cinnamon stick
2¼ cups sugar

Grind almonds very finely in a food processor while adding a little water to produce a cream.

Pour 2½ quarts water into a saucepan, bring to the point of simmering, and remove from heat. Add 1 pinch salt, sliced lemon, and finally the almond cream. Add cinnamon stick, cover, and let stand for 2 hours at room temperature.

After 2 hours, add sugar and stir well until it has dissolved completely. Strain liquid through a cheesecloth and squeeze cloth to extract the most liquid possible. Repeat straining process until the liquid is smooth. Refrigerate for at least 2 hours before serving.

Horchata keeps several days in a bottle in the refrigerator. It's also delicious chilled in the freezer. True *horchata* is traditionally prepared in Valencia using small white nuts called *chufas*, the tubers of a tropical plant, but almonds are the correct substitute.

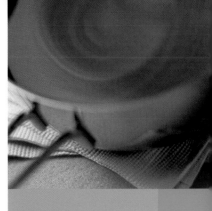

[catalan cream]

Pour milk and half-and-half into a saucepan. Slit open vanilla bean lengthwise, scrape out seeds with the tip of a knife, and add the seeds and the bean to the milk mixture along with the cinnamon. Slowly bring to a boil while stirring, then remove from heat and set aside.

In a large metal mixing bowl, beat whole eggs, egg yolks, and $1/3$ cup + 2 tablespoons sugar (reserve the rest of the sugar) with an electric mixer until you have an opaque and light yellow mixture.

Remove vanilla bean and cinnamon stick from the milk mixture. Slowly add milk mixture into egg mixture while beating.

Set mixing bowl with cream mixture over a pot that has about 2 inches of simmering water in the bottom. Keep the pot over low heat. Beat constantly for about 15 minutes (periodically scraping the bottom and sides) until the cream thickens. Distribute in 6 ramekins, let cool, and then refrigerate for 1 hour.

In the meantime, prepare the caramel: In a small saucepan, melt the remaining sugar ($2/3$ cup) and $2/3$ cup water until you have a brown caramel. Pour a thin, even layer of this liquid onto the surface of the cream in the ramekins. Place ramekins in the refrigerator and serve chilled.

Serves 6
Prep time: 40 minutes
Refrigeration time. 2 hours
Cooking time: 25 minutes

2 cups + 2 tablespoons whole milk
$1\frac{1}{4}$ cups half-and-half
1 vanilla bean
1 cinnamon stick
3 eggs + 4 egg yolks
1 cup + 2 tablespoons superfine sugar

Serves 4–6
Prep time: 30 minutes
Cooking time: About
2 hours
Refrigeration time: 4 hours

1 cup + 2 tablespoons
sugar
1¼ cups fresh pineapple
juice (or bottled juice)
4 eggs

[pineapple flan]

In a small saucepan, melt ¼ cup of the sugar with a few drops of water and heat until you have a brown caramel. Pour caramel into a small nonstick charlotte mold or a ceramic bowl and tilt it in every direction to cover the bottom. Set aside.

Combine pineapple juice and remaining sugar. Simmer over low heat, stirring occasionally until reduced by half. Let cool.

Using an electric mixer, beat eggs until thick and foamy. Pour syrup over the eggs in a thin and continuous stream while continuing to beat. Pour this mixture into the mold and seal tightly with aluminum foil. Place mold in a saucepan of barely simmering water (don't let it touch the bottom— make sure it's raised up a bit using a small metal rack as an aid). Cook for 90 minutes with the water simmering very gently until the mixture has set well. Let cool and refrigerate for several hours.

Just before serving, run a knife blade between the flan and the side of the mold and reverse flan quickly onto a plate. To serve this as a tapa, serve small quantities (it's a very sweet dessert) in individual cups in which you first poured a little half-and-half.

[brown sugar cream]

Bring milk to the simmering point with 1 tablespoon of the brown sugar and the lemon zest. Remove from heat and let cool for 5 minutes.

Beat together egg yolks, remaining brown sugar, and the flour. First pour a little of the milk mixture over the egg yolk mixutre while whisking, then continue adding gradually. Next, simmer over low heat while stirring constantly. When the cream thickens and coats the spatula, remove from heat.

Strain out the lemon zest and then pour cream through a chinoise or fine mesh strainer. Distribute in bowls. Let cool and then refrigerate for at least 1 hour. Serve very cold, sprinkled with cinnamon.

Serves 4
Prep time: 30 minutes
Cooking time: About
15 minutes
Refrigeration time: At least
1 hour

4 cups + 1 tablespoon milk
3 tablespoons brown sugar
Zest of 1 lemon
3 egg yolks
2 teaspoons flour
Ground cinnamon

Serves 6
Prep time: 10 minutes
Cooking time: About
15 minutes

8 ounces chocolate
couverture (specialty store)
4 cups + 1 tablespoon milk
2 teaspoons cornstarch

[spanish hot chocolate]

Break chocolate into little pieces and place in a saucepan with the milk. Heat slowly while beating constantly with a wire whisk until it simmers. Remove from heat. **D**issolve cornstarch in a little cold water, add this mixture to hot chocolate, and continue simmering over low heat while gently whisking until it thickens. Serve while hot.

Traditionally, this hot chocolate is served with *churros*, Spain's cinnamon crullers. Spanish hot chocolate prepared according to these instructions can be a delicious conclusion to a tapas meal.

[nut cake]

Serves 6–8
Prep time: 30 minutes
Cooking time. 1 hour

2¼ cups flour
2 teaspoons baking powder
8 ounces (16 tablespoons;
2 sticks) melted butter
1 cup + 2 tablespoons
sugar
3 eggs
1⅔ cups chopped walnuts
⅓ cup (scant) brandy
(Spanish if possible)

Sift flour with baking powder. Beat together melted butter and sugar until sugar is well dissolved. Gradually add flour mixture; then add eggs one by one. Mix carefully. Crush walnuts coarsely and mix with brandy. Add all this to the batter and combine.

Preheat oven to 350°F. Butter and flour a cake pan, pour in batter, and bake for about 1 hour. If the cake browns too quickly, reduce the temperature slightly.

Test doneness by piercing the cake with a knife blade (or wooden skewer). The piercing implement should come out clean. Remove cake from pan and let cool before serving.

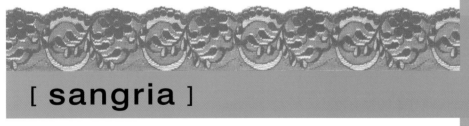

[sangria]

Makes 1 about quart
(6 servings)
Prep time: 20 minutes
Refrigeration time: At least
2 hours, ideally more

1 whole orange
1 lemon or lime
1 white or yellow peach
(in season), optional
3 cups fruity red wine
(e.g., Rioja)
1 cup Perrier (or other
sparkling water)
⅓ cup brandy (optional)
⅔ cup freshly squeezed
orange, mandarin orange,
or grapefruit juice
⅓ cup freshly squeezed
lemon or lime juice

Rinse orange and lemon or lime. Dry well and slice. Peel peach and cut into cubes or slices. Combine wine, Perrier, brandy (if using), and citrus juices.

Mix well, pour into a pitcher, add fruit, stir gently, and refrigerate.

You can vary this drink by replacing the peach with a pear or apple.

Brandy is not required. For a party, you should prepare two pitchers of sangria: a small one without brandy for the drivers and a larger one with brandy.

Here's a delicious version of a univerally-appreciated dessert that can be served hot or cold. The best rice for this recipe is the round type from the Valencia region or Italian arborio rice (which requires more milk).

[milk rice]

In a saucepan, bring 2 quarts of water to a boil and cook rice over high heat for 3 minutes while stirring well. Drain and rinse under cold water. Set rice aside in a colander.

Bring milk to a boil with half-and-half, cinnamon stick, and lemon or orange peel section. Add drained rice, butter, sugar, and salt. Boil vigorously for 5 minutes, then reduce heat to the minimum, cover, and simmer for about 1 hour. However, after 20 minutes, check how much milk has evaporated. If the rice seems too dry, add some hot milk. This dessert is ready when the rice grains are well separated and the sauce is thick and creamy.

Remove cinnamon stick and citrus peel. Pour rest into a shallow bowl and let cool completely. Then refrigerate for at least 2 hours. Serve chilled in individual portions, sprinkled with ground cinnamon.

You can add a regional flair to this recipe, making it Galician style, by sprinkling the hot rice with a layer of brown sugar and caramelizing it under the broiler. In this case, the milk rice can be served hot, warm, or cold.

Serves 4
Prep time: 30 minutes
Cooking time: About
1 hour
Refrigeration time: 2 hours

¾ cup long grain rice
4 cups whole milk
¾ cup + 2 tablespoons
half-and-half
1 cinnamon stick
2 inch section of orange
or lemon peel (minus any
white pith)
1½ tablespoons butter
1 cup + 2 tablespoons
sugar
1 pinch salt
Ground cinnamon

[anise cookies]

Makes 10–12 cookies
Prep time: 45 minutes
Cooking time: 30 minutes

1¼ cups powdered sugar
1 egg yolk
1 teaspoon fresh
lemon juice
2 teaspoons brandy
2¾ cups flour
1 large pinch salt
½ teaspoon ground
green anise seed
½ teaspoon ground
cinnamon
1 teaspoon finely grated
lemon zest
½ cup + 1 tablespoon
soft butter

In a small bowl, beat together 1 teaspoon of the powdered sugar, the egg yolk, lemon juice, and brandy. Set aside.

In a large bowl, mix flour, salt, ground anise seed, cinnamon, and grated lemon peel.

Using an electric mixer, beat butter until creamy. Fold in the egg yolk-lemon juice mixture (from the small bowl) as well as half the flour mixture while beating constantly. Then fold in remaining flour mixture using a spatula or wooden spoon.

Preheat oven to 300°F.

Roll out the dough thickly. This recipe makes 10–12 cookies and you should use an oval or round cookie cutter that is about 3 inches in diameter. Arrange cookie cutouts on a baking sheet and bake for about 30 minutes. They should be firm to the touch and slightly browned. Let cool for 2 minutes, then sift remaining powdered sugar over a sheet of baking parchment. Roll cookies in sugar and arrange on a serving platter. Sprinkle with remaining powdered sugar. Let cool. These cookies keep well but are very crumbly.

[orange cake]

Serves 6–8
Prep time: 30 minutes
Cooking time: 50 minutes

2 large oranges with
a thin peel
4 eggs
1⅓ cups sugar
1 cup + 1 tablespoon
olive oil
2¾ cups flour
2 teaspoons baking powder
1 pinch salt
1½ tablespoons butter

Preheat oven to 425°F. Rinse and scrub oranges. Cut into quarters while saving any juice and not removing peels. Remove any visible seeds.

Place orange quarters and juice in a food processor and blend until the oranges are reduced to a purée. Pour into a large bowl and add eggs, sugar, and olive oil. Beat well to obtain a uniform mixture.

In another large bowl, combine flour, baking powder, and salt. Fold this mixture into the orange mixture to form a smooth batter. Butter and flour a cake pan. Pour batter into pan and bake for 40–50 minutes. Remove from pan and let cool.

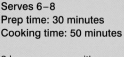

[sweet almond soup]

Serves 4–6
Prep time: 30 minutes
Cooking time: 20 minutes

1 cup blanched
skinless almonds
4 cups whole milk
7 tablespoons sugar
Zest of 1 lemon
½ teaspoon ground
cinnamon

In a mortar or food processor, crush almonds until you have a smooth paste. Add a little milk and mix with the almond paste. Add remaining milk and mix well.

Pour into a saucepan and add the sugar while gently folding. Add lemon zest. Bring to a boil over low heat while stirring constantly. Simmer for 20 minutes while stirring constantly with a wooden spatula.

Remove from heat, strain, and distribute almond soup in small individual bowls or teacups. Serve hot, sprinkled with cinnamon.

Finely blend tomato juice, orange juice, lime juice, onion, sugar, salt, chile pepper, and Tabasco. Pour into a pitcher and refrigerate. Serve in small glasses accompanied by tequila, sea salt, and lime wedges.

You're supposed to alternate between drinking sangrita and tequila along with biting into a lime wedge sprinkled with salt. You can also mix the tequila into the sangrita and serve it in glasses dipped in sea salt with ice cubes, a few slices of lime, and a celery stick. This Mexican cocktail can be served at the beginning of a tapas meal.

Prep time: 15 minutes
Refrigeration time: At least
1 hour

2¼ cups tomato juice
1 cup orange juice
¼ cup lime juice
1 tablespoon minced
white onion
½ teaspoon sugar
½ teaspoon salt
1 teaspoon fresh, finely
chopped green or red chile
pepper or hot *pimentón*
1 dash Tabasco
Lime wedges
Tequila (optional)

[sangrita]

You can either choose beverages to go with your tapas

buffet or you can choose tapas to go with the drinks you

serve. Take your cue from Latin America and serve

cocktails like sangrita. Fruity wines go well with light

tapas, especially tapas that don't contain too much

vinegar. Sherry is ideal with the more substantial dishes,

cured meats, and desserts.

[almond cookies]

Makes 24 cookies
Prep time: 30 minutes
Cooking time: 15–20
minutes

1²/₃ cups whole blanched
skinless almonds
2 egg whites at room
temperature
1²/₃ cups powdered sugar
1 teaspoon vanilla extract

Preheat oven to 350°F. Toast almonds lightly in the oven. In a mortar or food processor, reduce almonds to a very fine paste. Set aside.

Beat egg whites into peaks that are stiff but not rigid, then gradually fold in powdered sugar while continuing to beat. After adding sugar, beat for another 8 minutes. With a rubber spatula, mix one quarter of the egg whites into the almond paste gently, and then add the rest. Add vanilla extract.

Cover baking sheet with buttered baking parchment paper. Spacing them regularly, place spoonfuls of cookie mixture on the sheet, giving them a round shape. Bake in the oven for 15–20 minutes until cookies start to brown. Remove from oven. When hot, the cookies are soft, but they harden as they cool. Let cool and serve.

[christmas tartlets]

Serves 6
Prep time: 35 minutes
Cooking time: 25 minutes

1 pound pie dough
(purchased variety)
5 eggs
1¾ cup + 2 tablespoons
sugar
½ cup + ½ tablespoon
butter, melted
1 pinch salt
1 teaspoon genuine vanilla
extract
1⅔ cups chopped walnuts
⅔ cup raisins

Preheat oven to 350°F. Roll out pie dough into a thin sheet and use to line 6 miniature pie or tart tins, 6 ramekins, or a muffin tin, allowing pastry to overlap the edges slightly. If your tins are smaller, feel free to use them and make more tartlets. Refrigerate.

Beat eggs and sugar with a wire whisk (or electric mixer) until the mixture becomes creamy and light yellow. Add warm melted butter, salt, and vanilla extract. Mix well.

Combine walnuts and raisins and fill the pastry-lined ramekins halfway with this mixture. Add egg-butter mixture until tins are two-thirds full. Bake for 20–25 minutes until the edges of the pastry are slightly brown and the filling has solidified. Serve warm or cold.

The number of tartlets produced depends on the size of the tins.

[glossary]

Chile peppers: Spain brought back an infinite variety of chile peppers from the New World, which are available in powdered form as hot or sweet *pimentón* (smoked Spanish paprika). The red pepper of Espelette (translated in this book as spicy red chile pepper), is starting to appear in specialty grocery stores and is ideal for this type of cuisine.

Wines: Tapas were originally intended to accompany wine. Try out the astonishing Spanish wines, from the reds of La Mancha to the strong wines of Jerez (sherries). Rioja, with its oaky flavor, has a great deal of depth, as does valdepeñas, another Appelation d'Origine Contrôlée wine (Tempranillo is the varietal). The sherries, including *finos, amontillados,* and *olorosos*, go well with any flavor and even with desserts. The Ribera del Duero region also produces quality reds. The name *rueda* designates sophisticated whites. Penedés in the northeast is famous for its whites but even more for its *cavas* (Spanish sparkling wines).

Cured meats: You can find serrano ham of variable quality in the United States. The best Spanish ham is expensive, produced from local black-hoofed pigs (*pata negra*). The famous *jabugo* should be served alone in small slices with very good wine. As for chorizo, it takes many forms—more or less dry, more or less spicy, needing to be cooked, or ready to eat.

Olive oil: Spain's extra virgin olive oils are becoming more available in the United States. All the regions (Catalonia, Tarragona, Jaén, and Córdoba in Andalusia) produce high-quality oil, but Andalusian oils are especially full-bodied.

Cheese: Spain is rich in traditional cheeses, predominantly those made from ewe's and goat's milk. Look for manchego and perhaps Zamorano and Cabrales (which might be harder to find). You can substitute any blue cheese for Cabrales and, if you can't find manchego, use a good ewe's milk Pyrénées or a rustic white Cheddar.

[shopping hints]

Few of the Spanish products indispensable for the tapas recipes presented here will be difficult to find. They're available at specialty supermarkets and gourmet retailers. Also, seek out a Spanish import food shop—many carry Iberian products which are suitable for the recipes in this book.

appendices

[index of recipes]

Allioli potatoes 15
Almond cookies 114
Almond horchata 98
Andalusian gazpacho 45
Anise cookies 109

Basque bell pepper omelette 37
Beet and anise seed salad 62
Bell peppers Cadiz style 57
Brown sugar cream 102

Calamari fries 18
Carrot salad with cumin 76
Castilian-style garlic soup 79
Catalan cream 100
Cheese fritters 58
Chervil mussels 68
Chicken croquettes 24
Chicken in garlic sauce 34
Chicken in sparkling wine 18
Chicken pepitoria 37
Chorizo marinated in white
  wine 75
Christmas tartlets 115
Cream of gazpacho 48
Crispy fish fillets 65

Dates stuffed with chorizo 49
Dried fruit marmalade 79

Fillet of sole with pine nuts
  and raisins 76
Four-tiered omelette 14
Fresh fish "pil pil" 36
Fried cheese 26
Fried potato balls 71
Fried potatoes with a tomato
  sauce 40

Galician scallops Saint
  Jacques 54
Galician-style octopus 84
Garbanzo bean salad 88
Garbanzo beans in onion
  sauce 82
Garlic mushrooms 28
Garlic shrimp 16
Garlic, tomato, and serrano
  ham bread 33
Grilled tuna with marinated
  tomatoes 66

Lemon cream 97
Little seafood pockets 20

Manchego with quince paste 60
Mandarin orange monkfish 87
Marinated anchovies 29
Marinated eggplant 39
Marinated pork skewers 81
Meatballs and tomato sauce 42
Meatballs in an almond saffron
  sauce 78
Milk rice 106
Mini cheese and chile pepper
  soufflés 56
Monkfish packets 60
Mushrooms stuffed with
  serrano ham 88
Mussels escabèche 46

Nut cake 104

Orange cake 110

Pearl onions in sherry vinegar 54
Pears with blue cheese and
  sage 90

Pineapple flan 101
Pork fritters 12
Pork spareribs in garlic sauce 59
Potato "tortilla" 23
Potatoes with cheese and chile
  peppers 92

Quail "a la plancha" 93

Sangria 104
Sangrita 112
Sauce romesco 17
Savory chicken liver flan 70
Seafood cocktail 28
Seville olives 38
Shrimp "in raincoats" 15
Small salt-cod and raisin
  turnovers 53
Spanish hot chocolate 103
Spicy roasted pepper salad 48
Stuffed calamaris in their own
  ink 57
Stuffed chile peppers 42
Sweet almond soup 110

Tomato and green pepper
  salad 11
Tuna "meatballs" in white wine 80

[table of contents]

Spring 8
Tomato and Green Pepper
 Salad 11
Pork Fritters 12
Four-Tiered Omelette 14
Allioli Potatoes 15
Shrimp "in Raincoats" 15
Garlic Shrimp 16
Sauce Romesco 17
Calamari Fries 18
Chicken in Sparkling Wine 18
Little Seafood Pockets 20
Potato "Tortilla" 23
Chicken Croquettes 24
Fried Cheese 26
Garlic Mushrooms 28
Seafood Cocktail 28
Marinated Anchovies 29

Summer 30
Garlic, Tomato, and Serrano
 Ham Bread 33
Chicken in Garlic Sauce 34
Fresh Fish "Pil Pil" 36
Basque Bell Pepper Omelette 37
Chicken Pepitoria 37
Seville Olives 38
Marinated Eggplant 39
Fried Potatoes with a Tomato
 Sauce 40
Stuffed Chile Peppers 42
Meatballs and Tomato Sauce 42
Andalusian Gazpacho 45
Mussels Escabèche 46
Spicy Roasted Pepper Salad 48
Cream of Gazpacho 48
Dates Stuffed with Chorizo 49

Fall 50
Small Salt-Cod and Raisin
 Turnovers 53
Galician Scallops Saint
 Jacques 54
Pearl Onions in Sherry
 Vinegar 54
Mini Cheese and Chile Pepper
 Soufflés 56
Stuffed Calamaris in Their
 Own Ink 57
Bell Peppers Cadiz Style 57
Cheese Fritters 58
Pork Spareribs in Garlic Sauce 59
Monkfish Packets 60
Manchego with Quince Paste 60
Beet and Anise Seed Salad 62
Crispy Fish Fillets 65
Grilled Tuna with Marinated
 Tomatoes 66
Chervil Mussels 68
Savory Chicken Liver Flan 70
Fried Potato Balls 71

Winter 72
Chorizo Marinated in White
 Wine 75
Fillet of Sole with Pine Nuts
 and Raisins 76
Carrot Salad with Cumin 76
Meatballs in an Almond Saffron
 Sauce 78
Dried Fruit Marmalade 79
Castilian-Style Garlic Soup 79
Tuna "Meatballs" in White
 Wine 80
Marinated Pork Skewers 81
Garbanzo Beans in Onion
 Sauce 82

Galician-Style Octopus 84
Mandarin Orange Monkfish 87
Mushrooms Stuffed with Serrano
 Ham 88
Garbanzo Bean Salad 88
Pears with Blue Cheese and
 Sage 90
Potatoes with Cheese and Chile
 Peppers 92
Quail "a la Plancha" 93

Desserts & Beverages 94
Lemon Cream 97
Almond Horchata 98
Catalan Cream 100
Pineapple Flan 101
Brown Sugar Cream 102
Spanish Hot Chocolate 103
Nut Cake 104
Sangria 104
Milk Rice 106
Anise Cookies 109
Orange Cake 110
Sweet Almond Soup 110
Sangrita 112
Almond Cookies 114
Christmas Tartlets 115

Glossary 116
Shopping Hints 117
Index of Recipes 118

Published originally under the title: bar à tapas, © 2000 HACHETTE LIVRE (Hachette Pratique)
English translation for the U.S. and Canada © 2003 Silverback Books, Inc.

Food editor: Kelsey Lane

Managing editors: Suyapa Audigier & Brigitte Éveno

Reader: Elizabeth Penn

Artwork and creation: Guylaine & Christophe Moi

Production: Patty Holden & Nathalie Lautout

Editorial office: Sylvie Gauthier

Object photography: Matthieu CsechCover photo: Rapho / Alain Soldeville

Photos: Page 10 Marco Polo / F. Bouillot, page 32 Diaf / Lerault, page 52 Rapho / Alain Soldeville, page 74 Scope / Noël Hautemanière, page 96 Scope / Pascale Desclos

Printed and bound in Singapore

ISBN: 1-930603-82-7